Irving

THE TRUTH ABOUT

Dr. Jon M. Jenkins

P.O. Box 177

Gaylord, Michigan 49734

989.732.5676

www.echoespublications.com

© Copyright 2006 Echoes Publications
2nd Edition 2006
3rd Edition 2007
4th Edition 2008

ISBN: 1-933594-29-2

This book, or any portion thereof, may not be reproduced in any form without written permission from Echoes Publications

Printed in the U.S.A.
Color House Graphics, Grand Rapids, Michigan

For more information about titles printed by Echoes Publications, please contact
Grace Baptist Church
989.732.5676
www.echoespublications.com

TABLE OF CONTENTS

ACKNOWLEDGEMENTS . . . . PAGE 7

INTRODUCTION . . . . PAGE 8

1. THE PRINCIPLE EXPLAINED . . PAGE 11
Satan shows us temporal delights without showing us eternal dangers.

2. THE PRESENCE OF EVIL . . . . PAGE 41
Satan is the tempter behind every temptation.

3. PRAYING EARNESTLY . . . . . . PAGE 73
Prayer provides the strength to resist temptation.

4. THE POWER OF ENDURANCE . . PAGE 105
Abiding in Christ turns weakness under pressure into victorious resolve.

5. THE PITIFUL EXAMPLE . . . . PAGE 135
Samson's life is a tragic example of failure in temptation.

6. THE PROBLEM EXPERIENCED . . PAGE 167
The struggle with the flesh is the heart of the problem.

7. THE PATTERN EXHIBITED . . PAGE 193
Jesus' life is a triumphant example of success in temptation.

8. PREVAILING EMBRACED . . . PAGE 221
Let us embrace the victory that Christ has already won.

ABOUT THE AUTHOR . . . . PAGE 246

Acknowledgements

This project truly has been a team effort. I would like to thank the following people who contributed so much of their time and energy for the completion of this project.

Jessica Moody and Jeremy Goldsborough, who type-set and spent hours detailing every aspect of this volume.

Amanda Vest, who transcribed the material for this manuscript.

Pastor Robert Perrotti, Chad Vest, and Amanda Vest, who proofread and sharpened every word.

Greg Rood and Jeremy Goldsborough, whose graphic design enhanced this publication.

Introduction

Let me begin by being very transparent. God laid this study of temptation on my heart for personal reasons. I did not start studying this subject because I thought I would preach or teach it to my church members but because I wanted some answers to some old problems in my own life. There were some areas I simply wanted to conquer on my own. However, as I began to explore this topic, I read and checked a number of sources and found very little on the subject. Maybe so little has been written about temptation because very few have felt qualified to teach on it. Regardless, that is what inspired me to go deeper in studying – for my own benefit and because of the dearth of material.

As God began to show me some insight and victory, I felt I could not keep it to myself. That is not to say I feel as though I am an expert in the field of conquering temptation. I am just a sinner saved by grace and am growing in the knowledge of that grace every day, but I am not going to stop delivering a message just because I need it too. I remember hearing Bro. Lester Roloff say in a college chapel service many years ago, "I can never lower my preaching to my own practicing. I have to preach the Word of God whether I am successful at obeying it all or not."

May I welcome you into my office for a series of personal counseling sessions. I must say I have had to prepare myself before this study not just with **Scriptural Potency to Deliver the Topic**, but with **Spiritual Protection to Defeat the Tempter!** I am about to unveil the strategies, plots, and schemes of the Wicked

One, and this can incur personal assaults. Without sounding too spooky, I learned this subject had to be approached on bended knee.

This may be one of the most important subjects I have ever studied. It will help Christians be **Victors Over Temptation** instead of **Victims Of Temptation**. It will **Preserve Our Way** and **Protect Our Walk** so we are not **Deceived By Foolishness** and **Doomed For Failure**. It will **Enable Us To See Clearly** the personal evil that is central to spiritual warfare and behind every temptation. It will also **Inspire Us To Pray Earnestly** – knowing how crucial this great weapon of our warfare is to defeat temptation.

This material is not merely to be studied but also to be applied. It is not only to be understood but also to be obeyed. It is not only to be read, but also it is to be used. It is not to increase knowledge alone, but to inspire action. With prayer and thoughtful study, I commend the following for your good and the good of the kingdom of God.

Jon M. Jenkins
Gaylord, Michigan – April 2005

1

THE PRINCIPLE EXPLAINED

Satan shows us temporal delights without showing us the eternal dangers.

Let no man say when he is tempted, I am tempted of God: for God cannot be tempted with evil, neither tempteth he any man: But every man is tempted, when he is drawn away of his own lust, and enticed. Then when lust hath conceived, it bringeth forth sin: and sin, when it is finished, bringeth forth death. Do not err, my beloved brethren.
James 1:13-16

This chapter will lay a foundation for the proceeding chapters. Some of what you will read I have never read before. I believe you will find some tidbits in this study that will help you get victory over things you have been battling for decades. I do not know how you feel, but I am sick and tired of the devil's winning so many rounds in my life. I do not want him to continue to make me a laughingstock in the midst of the damned. I want him to go home with his tail between his legs and say, "We lost!

That rascal figured out what we were up to and has licked us at our own game!"

The Scripture says in James 1:16, *"Do not err . . ."* If the devil defeats me in temptation, then I erred. The old 1828 Webster's dictionary gives several definitions for err: "To wander from the right way, to deviate from the true course or purpose, to miss the right way, in morals or religion to stray by design or mistake," or simply "to mistake or commit error." I prefer "to deviate from the path or line of duty." It has military significance.

If the devil wins the battle in the realm of temptation, I erred, I deviated from the line of duty, I was outmaneuvered. Many of us who battle with temptation (and we all do) are frustrated and think: "If I just tried harder, did better, and had more character, then I would win this fight." All of those things are important, but this battle is not about technique. It is about first understanding that we are involved in spiritual warfare. If we do not understand the nature of warfare, then we will get licked over and over again and convince ourselves that we have a hopeless, secret battle on our hands. Many, to some degree, have a secret battle that they are not winning, a *"besetting sin"* as God calls it. If we keep losing this "secret battle", we develop a "secret" or double life. We should all be weary of living secret lives.

I heard a tragic story of a song leader in a Baptist church who was leading a double life. His wife was smarter than he thought she was, and she hired a private investigator with a hidden camera in his glasses. He followed the man and caught him in a motel with another woman. When confronted by his pastor, the man denied every bit of it. His pastor then went to the VCR in his living room and put in the tape the private investigator had recorded. The man began to weep and said, "I have been battling this for years."

My heart goes out to anybody losing the battle, but we need to stop looking at temptation as though it is something that is just our *own* problem. *Everybody* is battling with temptation to some degree in his or her life. You might be battling lust while someone else is battling a critical spirit; they are both sin and temptations that can either be resisted or yielded to. It depends upon how you understand temptation.

What Is Temptation?

Temptation is a Middle English word derived from both the French and Latin during the thirteenth century. The dictionary defines it as follows:

Temptation:
1. The act of tempting or the state of being tempted, especially to do evil
2. To entice to do wrong by promise of pleasure or gain
The word *temptation* is a companion to the word *enticement*.

Enticement:
To attract artfully or cleverly by arousing hope or desire
The words *temptation* and *enticement* are synonymous with the words *lure, decoy,* and *seduce.*

page • 13

When we go fishing, we try to make the fishing lure look as much like the real thing as possible in order to tempt the fish. The fish is thinking about *getting* supper, not *being* supper. The fishing industry has studied the habits and weaknesses of fish to determine what the fish will and will not fall for; consequently, it has developed a lure that looks real to the fish. Understand that the enemy of our soul has studied human nature for 6,000 years. We can develop as much character and willpower as possible, but we will not outwit a 6,000-year warrior.

> **Temptation *has the same root meaning as* Temporal *and* temporary.**

This is the most important principle in this book: the word *temptation* comes from the same root word as the words *temporary* and *temporal*. These words are defined as "lasting for a limited time" and "relating to time as opposed to eternity", respectively. The devil does not want us to know this truth about the word *temptation.* He wants to steal that seed out of your heart, but do not let him steal it. From this hour on, from this day forward, establish a beachhead in your soul like Normandy on D-Day of old to reclaim the ground the devil has stolen from your life! Remember that the words *temptation, temporal,* and *temporary* have the same root meaning. Everything that constitutes temptation is short-term and short-lived; its sinful season of pleasure passes quickly.

The context of the word *temptation* in light of the Scriptures is even deeper than the dictionary definition. The Bible teaches that Satan shows you ***temporal delights*** without showing you the ***eternal dangers.***

We have to understand that we have an eternal foe that does not want us to think about the consequences of our decisions. Unfortunately, this type of thinking goes against the narrow-minded, typical fundamental

> *Satan shows us* **Temporal Delights** *without showing us the* **Eternal Dangers.**

Baptist viewpoint of today. We think that as long as we are saved, anything goes. In reality, many things in the Bible go against our thinking. For example, Paul said,

> *Know ye not that the unrighteous shall not inherit the kingdom of God? Be not deceived: neither fornicators, nor idolaters, nor adulterers, nor effeminate, nor abusers of themselves with mankind, Nor thieves, nor covetous, nor drunkards, nor revilers, nor extortioners, shall inherit the kingdom of God.* **I Corinthians 6:9 –10**

I read a sermon by Billy Sunday that said, "If you are a drunkard, you are going to hell. If you are an adulterer, you are going to hell. If you are a fornicator, you are going to hell. Do not talk to me about your profession of faith." Now, that goes against our modern theology, but that is what he said.

The Devil is such a liar. He shows us a temporary path, practice, or pleasure, and tells us to go ahead and do it without fear of eternal effects. He will show you a business deal in which you have a chance to be honest and earn a little money, or be dishonest and earn a lot of money. He says, "If you will take this path or perpetrate this practice, it will bring pleasure, and it will not effect you eternally." Remember, the word *temptation* comes from the same root word as the words *temporal* and *temporary*.

How many men have traded everything for almost nothing? Several years ago, I was preaching in a certain city. While I was there, the pastor drove me past a massive church property with a diamond-shaped auditorium. It was breathtaking. There was a great bell tower with crosses on it that jutted four or five stories into the air. There were literally acres of curbed parking lots. I asked the pastor what church it was, and he told me a name I knew well. The name of this church has always stuck in my mind because, while my dad was a student in Bible college, he would occasionally go hear the well-known pastor of this church. My dad said that this pastor was a great pulpiteer. One Sunday night, while he was a still a student, my dad walked the aisle and was saved. This church always intrigued me.

> **Temptation *is Satan's convincing you that a* temporal Path, Practice, or Pleasure *will not have* eternal effects.**

When I inquired as to how the church was doing, he said that it had "gone under." We went to see if we could get in, but we could not. A deacon finally let us in. He showed us a gorgeous, three thousand-seat auditorium that, although breathtaking, was empty. This deacon told us that the pastor was a great man of God. He remembered a time when there were 100 buses parked behind the auditorium, but now they were down to 200 in Sunday school. He said, "Our mortgage right now is about $60,000 a month. We owe over $7 million on this property. In about two weeks we are going to have a bank sale and lose the property. As our pastor aged, his successor-to-be was his son. He was a very talented young man. He came back here and became the pastor of our church, and our senior pastor became Pastor Emeritus. Not long after that, our new pastor was caught in some moral sin, and our church imploded."

I walked around that property, realizing that young man paid an awful high price for a night of pleasure. He paid an awful great price to satisfy his flesh to have this great ministry crumble and implode. Now, I do not mean to be critical of anyone or of any church. In fact, I have prayed for those folks. This story illustrates that there are a lot of people willing to risk everything for almost nothing because they were outmaneuvered by the devil in this area of temptation. He convinces us that the temporary pleasure derived from our sin will not have eternal consequences. How many people will be in hell one day whose blood will be on the hands of those who allowed that great ministry to implode? I sure am glad he did not do it before my dad was saved there.

It is no wonder that Proverbs 4:26 says, *"Ponder the path of thy feet, and let all thy ways be established."* It is no mystery that Proverbs 5:3 states,

> *For the lips of a strange woman drop as an honeycomb, and her mouth is smoother than oil: But her end is bitter as wormwood, sharp as a twoedged sword. Her feet go down to death; her steps take hold on hell. Lest thou shouldest ponder the path of life, her ways are moveable,*

that thou canst not know them.

The wise man of Proverbs says, in effect, to the young men of this world, "Be sure you weigh your decisions carefully. There are eternal consequences to your temporary decisions." I may never be famous, but I sure do not want to be an illustration like I just gave. I may never be all I could be, but I do not want to be a "castaway" as I Corinthians 9:27 describes: *"But I keep under my body, and bring it into subjection: lest that by any means, when I have preached to others, I myself should be a castaway."* I may never fulfill my complete potential, but I do not want to be *"a proverb and a byword"* because the devil convinced me that a ***temporary pleasure*** was worth ***eternal damnation***.

Like Israel of old, Christians once used of God can become a shocking source of shame upon ***giving in to the work of Satan*** instead of ***giving over to the work of the Spirit.*** See how "erring" Jews became a public mockery – a *"proverb and byword"* in these verses:

And thou shalt become an astonishment, a proverb, and a byword, among all nations whither the LORD shall lead thee. **Deuteronomy 28:37**

Then will I cut off Israel out of the land which I have given them; and this house, which I have hallowed for my name, will I cast out of my sight; and Israel shall be a proverb and a byword among all people. **I Kings 9:7**

Then will I pluck them up by the roots out of my land which I have given them; and this house, which I have sanctified for my name, will I cast out of my sight, and will make it to be a proverb and a byword among all nations.
II Chronicles 7:20

To avoid this frightful ending to a fruitful life, I submit the following regarding temptation:

TEMPTATION IS A UNIVERSAL PROBLEM
"But every man is tempted..."

1. Temptation Is Personal

Someone once said, "I don't struggle with temptation; I just yield to it." Temptation is everywhere. The issue is not *if* you struggle with temptation; the issue is *what* your temptation is and how you handle it. One person is tempted with alcohol while another is tempted with a gossiping tongue. They are both wicked, and it is just as wrong to yield to the temptation to gossip as it is to yield to the temptation to drink alcohol. Everybody has his or her own "pet" sin. You may not like your pet sin, but you have not done anything with it.

Temptation is a personal thing. There are some things that do not tempt me that tempt you. There are some things that do not tempt you that tempt me. Let us admit that we all need to understand how to outmaneuver the devil in this realm of temptation. We can guarantee that our temptation will be tailor-made to match our weaknesses.

2. Temptation Is Universal

Temptation is not only personal, but it is also universal. We will never get spiritual or separated enough to prevent it. In Matthew 4:1-3, Jesus was *"led up of the Spirit into the wilderness to be tempted of the devil. And when he had fasted forty days and forty nights, he was afterward an hungred. And the tempter came."* There was nobody more spiritual or separated than Jesus, and if *He* had to endure temptation, we are fools to think we can avoid it.

Here, on this point of separation, is where many Christian school and home-school parents get sucker-punched when their children turn eighteen or nineteen. Many have thought all they had to do was have a spiritual family and be separated to have their children turn out right. There is a delusion in thinking you can actually *prevent* temptation by being separated. Separation is good. It is right. It provides strength and stability to your testimony, but it is not a preventative cure-all for the disease of temptation. Your children are going to be tempted; and, in fact, they are being tempted right now.

> *You will never be Separated Enough or Spiritual Enough to prevent temptation.*

3. Temptation Is Internal

Being more separated is not the answer. You can get so separated that you wear a robe and live in a monastery; but your temptation then would be pride. An old joke goes like this: A patient comes into a doctor's office and says, "Doc, I broke my arm in two places." The doctor's answer was, "Then stay out of those two places!" That sounds like good and simple advice, but the problem is that, when it comes to temptation, those places are *in* us, not *outside* of us. Temptations are predicated on our personal weaknesses. We *all* have lusts and specific temptations with which we deal internally on a daily basis.

TEMPTATION IS AN UNVEILED PROBLEM
*"But every man is tempted, **when he is drawn away**. . ."*

To be *"drawn away"* is to be *lured from the safety of self-restraint to sin*. The world, the flesh, and the devil are constantly trying to attract our attention and draw us away. The *New Bible Dictionary* puts it like this: "Satan tempts God's people by manipulating circumstances within the limits that God has allowed him in an attempt to make them desert God's will." That is why James 1:13 says, *"Let no man say when he is tempted, I am tempted of God . . ."* Your temptation does not come from God. He may allow the devil to have access to you, but He is not the tempter. The unveiled problem is that we are being *"drawn away."*

1. *Temptation Itself Is Not Sin.*

"For we have not an high priest which cannot be touched with the feeling of our infirmities; but was in all points tempted like as we are, yet without sin" (Hebrews 4:15). My Saviour was battered by the allurement and temptations that I face, and He emerged from it victorious, which means that I can do the same. In His forty-day temptation, Jesus did not defeat the devil in the power of His *divine* nature but in the power of His *human* nature. If He had done otherwise, He could not have given us any hope to do the same. James 1:14 tells of the strong desire or lust of the human soul to acquire something to fulfill the flesh. The *flesh* is that part of human nature where all of our natural desires have free reign. God has given the normal desires of life to us, and they, in and of themselves, are not sinful. For example, if we never felt hunger and thirst, we would not eat and drink, and we would die. The desire to eat and drink is God-ordained. Without fatigue, the body would not rest and would fall apart. The desire to sleep is God-ordained to preserve us. Sexual intimacy is also God-ordained. Without it, the human race could not continue.

> *Jesus defeated the devil in the power of **His** human nature, which means that* **I can do the same.**

2. Sin Occurs When We Satisfy Our Desires Outside The Parameter Of God's Will.

At the point that we satisfy our desires outside the parameter of God's will, temptation becomes sin. For example, eating is normal; gluttony is sin. Sleep is essential; laziness is sin. Hebrews 13:4 says, *"Marriage is honourable in all, and the bed undefiled: but whoremongers and adulterers God will judge."* The world, the flesh, and the devil are the three arenas from which we feel the pull to be *"drawn away."* Each attempts to draw us away from that which is good, normal, right, and appropriate to pursue that which is bad, abnormal, wrong, and inappropriate.

The desire for a young man to want to have a girlfriend and to be physical with her is a God-ordained, God-created desire. If a college student does not *want* to kiss a girl, we will send him home; but if he *does* kiss a girl, we will send him home, too. There is nothing wrong with the desire. The problem is fulfilling the desire for temporary pleasure and risking eternal disaster.

3. The Secret To Defeating This Desire Is To Fight It Where It Begins, Not Where It Ends.

"But every man is tempted, when he is drawn away of his own lust and enticed" (James 1:14). We want to cut off the thing that draws us away, but we will not be able to stop the world, the flesh, or the devil from tempting us. Each of us is *"drawn away of his own lust."* In Revelation 2:4 Jesus is speaking to the church of

Ephesus and says, *"Nevertheless I have somewhat against thee, because thou hast left thy first love."* What Jesus had against this church was that they had **"left their first love."** Every man is tempted *"when he is **drawn away**"* from something.

As old-time, Bible-believing Christians, we know what is right. If we have been saved very long and under good instruction, we know what it is to be a good Christian – specifically in prayer, service to God, etc. We know we need to be good children, spouses, parents, friends, siblings, employees, or employers. That is all obvious. If we were honest, we would believe that and practice it.

However, when no one is watching, the world, the flesh, and the devil are always trying to convince us that if we can be drawn away from what is important for a while, there will not be any eternal consequences. We try to deal with temptation at its conclusion rather than at its source. We say that we just have to get victory over pornography or alcohol or a critical spirit, or whatever you struggle with. You cannot stop the world, the flesh, and the devil from tempting, but you can stop them from defeating you.

4. The Way To Handle The Devil Is To Settle Your Loyalty With God.

I John 2:19 states, *"They went out from us, but they were not of us; for if they had been of us, they would no doubt have continued with us: but they went out, that they might be made manifest that they were not all of us."* We have always applied that verse in a wicked way, but maybe it simply means that they were drawn away because they were not loyal enough.

A. The Strategy For Married People:

My wife and I have been married for twenty-two years. Whenever I receive an appreciative letter from a lady, I let my wife read it. I appreciate letters from lady church members that tell me they appreciate and love me, but I have my wife look at them because I know I am like anyone else – just one step away from being the biggest loser you ever saw in your life. As a younger preacher, I did not think that, but after over twenty years of serving God, I have figured out that I am as weak today as I was the day I got saved because I have an old nature that is still alive and well. That old man is not predictable. The only thing about him that *is* predictable is that he is completely unpredictable. He will put on a religious face and even allow me to think that I am doing well for four or five months. Then, he broadsides me because I thought I was doing better.

The only way that I can resist some woman trying to pull me away from my wife is to stay close to my wife and be loyal to her. Proverbs 5:15-19 tells men how to handle adultery:

> *Drink waters out of thine own cistern, and running waters out of thine own well. Let thy fountains be dispersed abroad, and rivers of waters in the streets. Let them be only thine own, and not strangers' with thee. Let thy fountain be blessed: and rejoice with the wife of thy youth. Let her be as the loving hind and pleasant roe; let*

her breasts satisfy thee at all times; and be thou ravished always with her love.

You do not handle temptation by fighting the devil; you handle temptation by getting so in love with your wife that when someone tempts you, you think, "What in the name of God is that? Trade treasure for a piece of trash? You might be younger or prettier than my wife, but you are not worth what you are going to cost me for eternity. I am going to be paying for you until eternity passes, and it is never going to pass. Thousands will die and go to hell; thousands will be corrupted and perverted and ruined. God will say, 'You did it one day - was it worth it?' No woman, no matter how beautiful, is worth all that pain and suffering." My wife and I are not perfect, but we have decided that we like each other. A good marriage is not one that never has battles; a good marriage is one that survives battles.

> *The only way that I can resist some woman trying to pull me away from my wife is to stay close to my wife.*

B. *The Strategy For Church Members:*

The devil may throw you a temptation that would pull you away from your church - perhaps a bowling league or some sport, or maybe a better job somewhere else. The point is not that God does not want you to enjoy life or prosper; but is it worth having twice as much fun and money while losing your children and your marriage? Temptation is not always immoral; it may just be trading something that is *best* for something that is *good*. We ought to get so involved in church and make it our life's work and source of friendship that we would not think of leaving it for a sports outing. We ought to be more loyal than that.

C. The Strategy For Young People:

Let me address young people directly. Do you understand that though your mom and dad are not perfect, they still pay the bills and supply the food? Be careful when someone or something tries to draw you away from your parents. Someone who pulls you away from your parents is not your friend. If you could see inside the glove that has reached out to you, you would see hell-scarred hands! Lucifer himself is using that person to pull you away from your parents. When your friends are gone, your parents will still be there. When all hell breaks loose, and you need a miracle, you will not be going to your friend for help. You will go see dad, and he will probably help you because he loves you and is loyal to you.

There is no girl or boy worth ruining your relationship with your parents. You need to have a revival of appreciation for, and loyalty to, your parents – even though they are old fashioned. Thank God that you do not have a couple of liberated idiots for parents who would let you sleep with your girlfriend in the living room. Thank God you have some old time parents who are trying to protect you – even if they appear foolish. Foolish is the young person that has traded the love and respect of mom and dad for a young lady or young man or friend and ended up in a roach-infested motel halfway across the country. Then they dial up mom and dad to see if they will give them a bus ticket back to the house. *That* is foolish.

In Detroit, Michigan, there was a teenage boy who beat his girlfriend's belly with a baseball bat to try to kill the baby he had put there so they did not have to face responsibility. I wonder if, while he was swinging the bat, she was saying, "I sure am glad you are my boyfriend." A young man took liberties he had no right to take; a young girl, because she wanted him to love her and did not want to lose him, gave him things she should have never dreamt about giving him. They got caught. You would think that when he proposed swinging a baseball bat at her belly she would have woken up. It is amazing the terrible things you will do when the world, the flesh, and the devil draw you away from your parents.

I will never forget several years ago when I preached in New York the Sunday after Thanksgiving. That Saturday, we took our children to see Manhattan. They had never seen it before, having been reared in the country. We went to FAO Schwartz toy store, the Empire State Building, and the big aircraft carrier on the Hudson River. After four or five hours, my middle son Brandon who was eight or nine at the time, tugged on my arm and said, "Dad, are we done yet? I don't like it here. It's too dirty." Walking past those alleys and seeing homeless people on the streets did not pass Brandon by. The glitz of Manhattan did not fool him. I thought they would be excited about it, but they all wanted to leave. In effect they were saying , "Give me little Northern Michigan. Give me the country. Give me my security, my world." I do not mean any disrespect to those who live in big cities; I am trying to illustrate a point about the world and being loyal to home. The devil is such a liar. He shows you the glitter when he is only trying to draw you away from the people most important in your world.

D. The Strategy For Preachers:

There was a temptation put in front of me a couple of years ago to leave Gaylord. A big opportunity was presented to me in another ministry of national acclaim, but I loved my church folks too much to leave. In some ways it would have been a great honor, but not as great an honor as pastoring the folks at my church. That offer was not big enough to draw me away. God knew, even though I did not know at the time, all the things He was going to allow our church to do. He allowed the devil to test me before He trusted me. I have no doubt that had I said *yes* to that temptation I would have been happy, but all the miracles that have happened in the last several years in my life and ministry would not have happened. The blessings of a college, thirty-five acres on I-75, and the Otsego Lake Baptist church building being given to our ministry, and on and on would not have happened. I made that decision because I was loyal to Grace Baptist Church and how much it meant to my heart.

E. The Strategy For Men:

Pornography is a strong allurement that the devil throws at men, especially in the day in which we are living. Every man knows what I am talking about. The source is not in the thing that *tempts* us; it is in the loyalty in the *relationship* that exists before the temptation – whether to our wives or our children.

I have sat in my office many times and looked at a beautiful, weeping lady who said, "I don't know what he saw in that pornography. Maybe it's my fault; maybe I didn't meet his needs." I have to control my temper, but I say, "Listen, dear lady, it has nothing to do with you. The reason he did it is because he is a pervert. That does not mean that he cannot be forgiven for it, but this is not about you." I cannot tell you how many precious ladies have been devastated to find out their husbands are hooked on pornography. Then they think, "Where did I fail? Was I not a good enough wife? Was I not submissive enough? Did I not meet his needs?" That has nothing to do with it, and many men who have battled with pornography will tell you that intimacy with their wife was not the issue. They say that they got hooked on a *temporary pleasure* without thinking of the *eternal consequences*, only to find themselves embarrassed, sitting in front of the preacher, and revealing their hidden world.

Men with a teenage daughter, God has put a young lady in your world. You are her hero, her dad, her king, and her protector. What is she going to think when she finds out you are a pervert? A man who looks at pornography is like a low man that crawls around in the gutter. My daughter is more important to me than a dirty magazine. I want her to want me to give her away at the wedding, not ask me out of duty. I am not mad at men who have fallen, but I do not know how men rationalize it. I have counseled men about this kind of sin and they have said, "Please don't tell my daughter. Whatever you do to me, please don't let my kids find out." They are saying that they cannot face their children finding out that they did not love them as much as they said they did.

Whatever the relationship in which we find ourselves, the quality, intimacy, and loyalty to one another must be preserved. Whether husband with wife, parent with child, Christian with church, friend with friend, etc., the strength of that relationship will determine the strength of our resistance to temptation. Many temptations are so strong because we are so weak. You cannot backslide from something you have never progressed toward.

5. *Every Temptation Is About Your Love, Not Your Lust.*

A. *With Adults:*

My goal is to love what I am lusting after and lust after what I love. It is not wrong for a man to lust after a woman if he is married to her. As a matter of fact, he needs to do that. You are prone to be tempted because you do not lust after the person you love. The word *lust* simply means "strong, personal desire." Do you think some twenty-year-old floozy with a messed-up background is going to cost me my wife just because she is cute? I am not going to trade the seasoned Christian woman God has given me for that. My love for my wife must be stronger than my lust for a another lady.

I was on an airplane where the stewardess was a little too friendly. She called me "honey." That might have been her way of being kind, but there was a part of me that did not understand

> ***Many temptations are So Strong because we are So Weak.***

being called "honey" by a woman other than my wife. I said, "I'm not your honey. The lady who gave me this ring is my honey, not you." She was rude to me the rest of the flight, but I did not care. Some of you men will go to the same restaurant time after time where there is a little waitress who flirts with you. If you do not allow anyone to call you "honey" or "sweetie," people might just think that your spouse is lucky. The world is looking for something real.

B. With Teenagers:

Young people, allow it to be the unspoken word in the youth group that you are loyal to your family. If somebody tries to get you to do wrong, tell him that you are going to knock his teeth out if he ever tries to do it again. You have a testimony to uphold. Do not have this testimony: "He sure is cool. He talks sort of dirty." Does it not offend you that others are trying to pull you away from your testimony, parents, church, preacher, and salvation? Do not allow people to mess with your testimony.

In both cases, adults or teenagers, others will not be offended if they see that you are loyal to your family, your Lord, your wife, your children, or your parents.

Temptation Is An Underlying Problem

*"But every man is tempted,
when he is drawn away of his own lust."*

While the **Unveiled Problem** is that Satan is trying to draw you away from that to which you should be attached, the ***Underlying Problem*** is that he is able to do it because he knows something about human nature. He knows that in every one of us is a fallen nature with desires inconsistent with our new nature's desires. In our text, James confirms what we already know to be true. Many of our temptations begin *inside* us. The temptations call from within us nearly every day. Often men have said, "I don't know what comes over me. I don't want to do it. I know it's not right, but it seems like all I think about some days." The underlying problem is *". . . of his own lust."* We have all had the experience of responding to that call. We have all failed to live up to not only God's standards but also our own standards as well.

1. The Underlying Problem Is Unadulterated Selfishness.

People do not care what it costs. They are willing to risk forever for one more fix, one more pleasure, and one more peak. Child of God, every one of our old natures has a gambler in its heart. We are willing to gamble our testimony that our husband, our wife, our parents, our preacher, or our grandmother will find out about our secret sin. Even though all those people matter to us, we are still willing to risk it for one more short-term, temporary, temporal, physical, or emotional high.

2. The Only Prescription Is Paying The Price.

Most people do not have enough character or a good enough

conscience to pay the price when no one is watching. Paul said in I Corinthians 9:27, *"But I keep under my body, and bring it into subjection: lest that by any means, when I have preached to others, I myself should be a castaway."* Where did Paul find the strength? II Corinthians 5:14 says, *"For the love of Christ constraineth us . . ."* That word *constraineth* means "to constrict, control or get a grip on." Paul simply said, "I love what I am tempted to be drawn away from more than what is drawing me away."

"Brethren, if a man be overtaken in a fault, ye which are spiritual, restore such an one in the spirit of meekness; considering thyself, lest thou also be tempted" (Galatians 6:1). The surest way to get caught in some immoral sin is to be critical of someone who was caught in some immoral sin. The devil is going to set you up, and God is going to burn you. He is going to make you the laughingstock of the world. Be careful of being critical of those who struggle; you will probably fall in the exact same area.

I know preachers who were ferocious when they found out another preacher had messed up. Two or three years later, you find out that they too are out of the ministry.

Dr. Lanny Hasbrook, who is in heaven now, said, "No sin embarrasses a preacher more than adultery. When a man gets proud, God will let the devil take him out with it because *'God resisteth the proud, but giveth grace unto the humble."* (James 4:6). Preachers should take a good stand and be firm, but they should not be critical. When people have fallen and stumbled, it is time for every one of us to help them get back up, *"considering thyself, lest thou also be tempted"* (Galatians 6:1).

Abraham loved Sarah, his wife of over one hundred twenty years. When she passed away, he was in a place called Ephron. He did not own any land there because he was just passing through, but he wanted to bury his wife in a place that could become a family memorial to which he could return. He did not want to be like a prisoner of war and just bury her in a ditch somewhere. He wanted to be able to come back and remember.

There was a Hittite who owned this land, and Abraham said to him, "I want to bury my wife here, and there is a cave at the end of this field that I have an interest in." Abraham was so respected that the Ephronites were willing to give it to him. They realized that Abraham was a man of God and had God's blessings on his life. They were honored that he wanted to bury his loved ones in their country, but Abraham would not accept their gift. If he was going to bury his wife there, he was going to pay for it. He did not want them to be able to take it away from him someday or think that they had a part in his blessings, as he had also told the king of Sodom years earlier. They told him the value of the land was four hundred shekels of silver, and Abraham paid it.

If you want victory and blessings, you have to pay the price. If you want to bury that besetting sin once and for all, then be like Abraham and pay for the land you have lost to the devil and kick him out. Do you want to bury that pornography, those cigarettes, that critical spirit, and that rebellious heart once and for all? Would you like to put the devil out of business in at least one area of your life? The devil comes along and says, "Hey, we have been friends for a long time. It doesn't bother me that you struggle. I'll even back off. I won't mess with you much here."

Do you think he is going to allow you to get victory for nothing? Every apple you will ever buy from the devil has a worm in it. Tell the devil that you are going to pay the price.

3. What Price Are You Willing To Pay To Get The Victory?

Are you willing to pay cable TV? Are you willing to pay Internet in your home? If you cannot handle it, quit playing games. Tell the devil, "This is my office, and there will never be pornography in here again. The only way I can guarantee that is to get rid of the Internet." If you have to have the Internet for employment, have your computer technician give all of the passwords to your wife.

There have been many times that I just skimmed by out of the devil's reach, and it looked like I was a great Christian. The truth was, it was due to some decisions I made a long time ago. I bought the land and paid the price. I made up my mind years ago that if God was going to allow me to travel the country and influence other churches, I had to stay right. Many men have traveled and gotten in trouble. I am aware of that danger, so I decided not to watch television in motel rooms. Sometimes I get lonely, and it would be nice to watch a little news or a documentary. I decided to pay the price in that area, and I have seen God use me in ways I cannot believe.

Recently, when I was leaving a church in which I was preaching, the pastor was weeping and said, "Brother Jenkins, could you give us another week? Could we keep the revival going? This has been a turning point in our lives." One deacon even said, "It is almost as if God sent you in His place." When I got back to my motel I said, "God, I am a filthy rotten sinner; I do not deserve people to say that about me. I hardly knew what to preach tonight, let alone have them tell me that it was almost as if God came by when I came by." It sure is awesome to be able to thank God for using me. It is worth television. Every once in awhile, I will want to check the weather when I am in a hotel room, and I call my wife to ask permission. It might sound crazy, but it sure helps me to stay straight.

> *I do not have convictions or standards because I am a good Christian; I have them because I am not.*

Young person, you might need to pay the price of a friend. You are so insecure and desire to be accepted so badly, you may accept someone that will greatly hinder you. Maybe you need to be called a "geek" or a "momma's boy" in order to pay the price. This is not because you *are* a good Christian but because you are *not* a good Christian. I do not have convictions and standards because I am a good Christian; I have them because I am not. You can keep fighting the temptation, but it would be better to fight the real battle.

Are you willing to purchase the land so you can put this temptation to rest? I do not know what you need to pay, give up, sacrifice, or surrender. Maybe it is higher dress standards, music standards, or greater accountability.

Accountability is crucial in the battle of temptation. For

example, I have never required our deacons to be in a certain number of services per year. I want them to be faithful out of desire, not out of constraint. However, our deacons frequently ask me if they can go out of town for vacation. In doing that, they are saying that they want to be accountable. You might think that you do not want anybody telling you what to do, but the devil is telling you what to do, and you are listening well. There is not one person that can live above accountability without getting in trouble.

People in a relationship need to be accountable to each other. This is true for children and parents, church members and leaders, but especially for husbands and wives. Spouses should not keep secrets from each other – no secret bank accounts, checking accounts, post office boxes, etc. If you are keeping things from your mate, it is because you are doing something wrong. What kind of sorry man would put his wife to bed and stay up and watch TV and play around with the Internet? People cannot handle staying up alone until one or two o'clock in the morning. Go to bed earlier and do not trust your flesh.

There was a lady whose husband was staying up until two or three in the morning night after night on the computer. She came to me and said, "Preacher, I think he's doing something wrong." I knew he was doing something wrong; there is nothing that he is doing on the Internet at two o'clock in the morning that is pleasing God. She knew enough about the computer that she did some research and busted him. He tried to convince her that it was not hurting their relationship. I told her that he was an idiot and that she needed to tell him that it was either her or the computer. He kept conning her.

One day he tried to turn on the computer, and it would not work. She said, "I have the motherboard, and I am not telling you where it is until you go talk to the preacher because I want it as evidence that you are not being honest." He got right with God. That man paid the price, stopped lying, and got help. So can you if you acknowledge these principles.

2

THE PRESENCE OF EVIL

Satan is the tempter behind every temptation.

"For this cause, when I could no longer forbear, I sent to know your faith, lest by some means the tempter have tempted you, and our labour be in vain."
I Thessalonians 3:5

"Then was Jesus led up of the Spirit into the wilderness to be tempted of the devil...And when the tempter came to him, he said, If thou be the Son of God, command that these stones be made bread." **Matthew 4:1**

In This chapter, we are going to examine the reality of spiritual warfare behind each temptation in various Bible verses.

THE PLAN OF SPIRITUAL WARFARE:

The Bible says in II Corinthians 2:11, *"Lest Satan should get an **advantage** of us: for we are not ignorant of his **devices**."*

The word advantage literally means, "to take advantage of us" while the word *devices* means "thoughts, tricks, or temptations." In most of our lives, this verse is not a true statement - we are ignorant of his temptations. As long as we are ignorant, Satan will be triumphant. The subject of spiritual warfare is both foreign and frightening because of the ignorance of God's people. When you hear someone like Brother Marvin Smith of Harvest Baptist Church in Fort Dodge, Iowa, most people think, "Whoa, that demonic possession and oppression - I don't know about getting carried away with all that stuff." That is exactly what the devil wants you to think and say. Satan is powerful, but his power is not unlimited. It is limited by the power of God. As long as Satan can keep Christians spooked about his power, he will stay victorious.

The Preparation For Spiritual Warfare

David understood spiritual warfare in Psalm 23:5, *"Thou preparest a table before me in the presence of mine enemies: thou anointest my head with oil; my cup runneth over."* The table that God spreads before the Christian is the Word of God. The Word of God is our provision for spiritual warfare. *"Thou anointest my head with oil,"* is talking about the Spirit of God. David said, "The Word of God is my **provision** in spiritual

> *As long as we are Ignorant, Satan will remain Triumphant!*

warfare, and the Spirit of God is my **protection** in spiritual warfare." But this great verse has at its centerpiece – *"in the presence of mine enemies."* The truth of the matter is, we live every day in the presence of our enemy. We will never conquer temptation if we are ignorant of the grim fact that our enemy is a daily presence.

THE PERSPECTIVE ON SPIRITUAL WARFARE

*"Then Jesus said unto the chief priests, and captains of the temple, and the elders, which were come to him, Be ye come out, as against a thief, with swords and staves? When I was daily with you in the temple, ye stretched forth no hands against me: but **this is your hour, and the power of darkness."*** **Luke 22:52**

Jesus said in effect, "Right now, between here and Calvary, is your hour. This is when you have the advantage. Right now is the hour of the power of darkness."

The distance you live from the Cross determines how much power you have in the world in which you are living. If you are not all you ought to be, it is because you are living in the "power of darkness."

Jesus understood that what

> *The Word of God is my Provision in spiritual warfare, and the Spirit of God is my Protection in spiritual warfare.*

was happening in the garden scene in Luke 22 was not physical warfare. That is why He told Peter to put his sword away. Let me hasten to say, Jesus was not then, nor is He now, against swords or guns. He told Peter to put it his sword away because the warfare in which they were presently engaged was spiritual, not physical. Incidentally, he said in Luke 22:36, "…he that hath no sword, let him sell his garment, and buy one." Just because we engage in spiritual warfare does not eliminate the existence of valid and justified physical warfare. I support the right to take up and bear arms for self-defense and the defense of justice and freedom around the world.

The Power Of Spiritual Warfare

Colossians 1:12-14 says, *"Giving thanks unto the Father, which hath made us meet to be partakers of the inheritance of the saints in light:* **Who hath delivered us from the power of darkness,** *and hath translated us into the kingdom of his dear Son: In whom we have redemption through his blood, even the forgiveness of sins."* If you are a heaven-bound child of God, you have been given the power to be delivered from the power of darkness. That does not mean that you are a victorious Christian, it means you can be. The devil wants us to stay as ignorant as possible about where we are in relation to the power of darkness.

Talking of His primary function of ministry, Jesus told Paul in Acts 26:18 that his job and our job is, *"To open their eyes, and to turn them from darkness to light, and from the power of Satan unto God, that they may receive forgiveness of sins, and inheritance among them which are sanctified by faith that is in me."* In contradiction to Christ, Satan wants you to think that your sin issue has never been totally resolved. That is why I have always been opposed to the principles of Alcoholics Anonymous (AA). I like the idea of helping folks, and there is nothing wrong with support groups, but the problem with AA is that there is never any permanent change or resolution. Whether you have been in AA one week, twenty weeks, or twenty years, every week that you stand up to give your testimony, you say, *"My name is John Doe, and I'm an alcoholic."* That is exactly what the devil wants you to say. *"I've got a pornography problem. I've got a lying problem. I've got a laziness problem."* Well I've got a problem with that thinking because the blood of Calvary has washed us!

"Unto him that loved us, and washed us from our sins in his own blood." **Revelation 1:5**

*"And such **were** some of you: but ye are washed, but ye are sanctified, but ye are justified in the name of the Lord Jesus, and by the Spirit of our God."* **I Corinthians 6:11**

"If any man be in Christ, he is a new creature: old things are passed away; behold, all things are become new." **II Corinthians 5:17**

In fact, the next time the devil wants to keep you in your place of defeat, remind him where he is going to be kept in defeat for all eternity! So, live on the victory side of Calvary.

We learned in chapter one that temptation is both internal and personal. *"But every man is tempted, when he is drawn away of his own lust, and enticed"* (James 1:14). In this chapter, we are also going to learn that temptation is infernal (spawned straight out of hell) and powerful. You are not battling with temptation – you are battling with the enemy of your soul. You say, *"Well, I can't get the victory over this or that."* If you could see behind the temptation, you would see the tempter.

THE PERSON BEHIND SPIRITUAL WARFARE

If someone who had AIDS running through his body was a virtual skeleton pushing an IV post hooked to his veins, and he offered you ladies a chance to be immoral with him, I think you would be able to walk away. But the devil will show you some hunk of a young man that everybody thinks is somebody. He will not show you the real enemy behind the temptation. Men, he shows us some young, lustful-looking lady. He does not show you a prostitute that is dying of AIDS on skid row. He does not show you somebody in a hospital ward with venereal diseases; because the devil always tries to hide the tempter behind the temptation.

Remember that *temptation* comes from the same root word as the words *temporal* and *temporary*. From a Biblical and technical viewpoint, **temptation** is:

- Satan convincing us that "a temporal path, practice, or pleasure has no eternal effects."

- Satan conveying "temporary delights without eternal dangers."

The problem is that he is a liar. The Bible says in Ezekiel 18:20, *"The soul that sinneth, it shall die."* When Adam and Eve heard the devil say, "Oh, you don't have to worry about that. You can eat that fruit. *Ye shall not surely die"* (Genesis 3:4). What he should have said was "yet." When Adam and Eve took that fruit, immediately some of their being began to decay. Death did not come to a *culmination* when they took that fruit, but it had an *inauguration* when they took the fruit. Just because we have *not yet* died does not mean we have gotten away with our sin. Just because you are not in a hospital right now dying of some disease does not mean you have gotten away with your sin.

> **Temptation is Internal and Personal and Infernal and Powerful!**

We do not have enough preaching on judgment anymore. We need more preaching on the judgment and wrath of God. All we hear in 21st century contemporary religion is that God is love. Thank God that He is love, but He is just as mad as He is glad. You had better thank God that He is dealing with most of us in grace and mercy. There is coming a day when God will pull the mask of grace off to deal with the world in wrath and judgment.

THE PRESENCE IN SPIRITUAL WARFARE:

Ephesians 6:12 says, *"For we wrestle* [to be engaged in a struggle with] *not against flesh and blood, but against principalities* [demons or fallen angels], *against powers, against the rulers of the darkness of this world, against spiritual wickedness in high places."* The devil wants you to think that the battle you are in is a purely physical battle when it is anything but physical. It is strictly a spiritual battle. We do not wrestle against pornography. We do not wrestle against lust. We do not wrestle against a bad thought life. We do not wrestle against drugs. We do not wrestle against alcohol. We do not wrestle against cigarettes. **We wrestle against the literal demons of hell.**

When men go to the grocery store and pick up a pack of nicotine sticks, it is a huge deal to the devil. He knows that as long as you are blowing smoke in people's faces, you will not be much of a soul winner. If it is so right to do, then why don't you wear them in your front pocket when you go to church? You know it is not right. There is no reason to even defend it. Do not tell me that you are hooked and cannot get loose. Some of you are still smoking nicotine sticks, not because you *cannot* get free but because you *do not want* to get free. You want to get right with God, but you do not want to have to give up everything.

I wish I could take you to the hospital I went to as a Bible college student on the corner of Division and Addison Avenues in northwest Chicago. I went to see one of my bus kid's grandfathers who was dying. He was outside sitting on a little wall when I saw him. He had a tracheotomy, which is a hole drilled in his neck to breathe, and he was smoking through that little hole because he could not get free. It was not pretty then. It will be embarrassing to bury a church worker or bus worker someday and find out they had lung cancer. You need to understand that you are not battling with nicotine – you are battling with the presence of evil. The devil knows that as long as he can keep you hooked, you are a poor testimony of a victorious Christian. You are, in effect, saying, "God had enough power to get me out of hell, but He did not have enough power to get hell out of me."

"For we wrestle . . . against powers. . . ." Powers is a word that means "authorities." It literally means that Satan's kingdom, just like God's, operates on a chain of command. Not only do we wrestle against *principalities*, meaning those lower level demons or fallen angels, but also against *authorities*, meaning those who instruct the demons. Notice God says, *"we wrestle . . . against the **rulers** of the darkness of this world."* Rulers are "lords and princes." He is describing a hierarchy as would be found in a military or governmental structure. He is describing a hierarchy of a well-organized enemy strategy.

Then He goes deeply into the battlefield we are in when He says, *"we wrestle. . . against spiritual wickedness in high places."*

Remember Isaiah 14:13-14,
"For thou hast said in thine heart, I will ascend into heaven, I will exalt my throne above the stars of God: I will sit also upon the mount of the congregation, in the

sides of the north: I will ascend above the heights of the clouds; I will be like the most High."

These verses are talking about the devil. When you are battling with temptation, you are not fighting a cigarette, a dirty magazine, a critical tongue, or a bitter spirit; you are fighting the devil and his generals and his majors and his colonels and his foot soldiers. Right now, they are strategizing for your tomorrow. The devil knows where you are going to be at ten o'clock and eleven o'clock and twelve o'clock and one o'clock and two o'clock and whether or not he is planning a rendezvous. You are going to walk into situations tomorrow where there will literally be an army of demons ready for you. You might want to get up and read your Bible tomorrow morning. You might want to get a hold of the God of your soul and make sure that God and the angels of heaven are on *your* side tomorrow.

Temptation is a daily skirmish in the great battle of spiritual warfare. Behind every temptation there lies, not just some*thing*, but some*one*. It is not just the *Presence Of Human Weakness* that causes us to fail in temptation; it is the **Presence of Evil**! The reason some *fail to resist the power of the temptation* is because we *fail to understand the person who is the tempter.* The reason some fall so quickly, and all of us fall more frequently than we should, is that we fail to understand that temptation is the **Presence of Evil.**

These are three main points of strategy in which we must engage the enemy of our soul – Satan himself.

WE MUST RECOGNIZE THE FOE

1. *He Is An Opposing, Universal, Eternal Foe.*

> *Jesus was not just facing a force of some anonymous evil; he was fighting a foe that is the very essence of evil!*

He has been fighting against everybody that claims to know God for all history. Jesus was not just **Facing a Force** of some anonymous evil, he was **Fighting a Foe** that is the very essence of evil. As long as the devil can get us to think we are fighting an anonymous evil, we will have a different attitude than if we knew it was literally him. You should almost be able to smell the sulfur under his breath when he is talking to you. As long as we do not see the death, disease, destruction and devil behind our temptation, we will never have the strength to say no.

I was reading a horrible article a few years ago in a book entitled <u>AIDS: What the Government Isn't Telling You</u>. The author was the head of trauma surgery at San Francisco General Hospital. She was not a Christian; as a matter of fact, she was sympathetic to the homosexual crowd. Yet even she said that the AIDS epidemic in America came from the homosexual bathhouses in San Francisco. She described how that in one night, some men would have thirty to forty homosexual partners. They would have blindfolds on so they would not see their partner. Men would walk around with IV carts, dying of AIDS, being immoral with these blinded partners. AIDS started with that ungodly, wicked perversion. There is not a man that would ever be unfaithful to his wife if he knew the woman with whom he was being unfaithful was dying of AIDS. The devil blinds, masquerades, and hides the tragedy of sin.

Young people, you may think you are fooling adults. You say, "I don't care what that preacher says." But the preacher is not the one you need to care about. You need to care about what the devil says, and he has declared that he wants you. There are some college students who are away from home for the first time and they cannot even be faithful to class. Some do not even make it a semester. If you think that you can mess around with sin, not walk with God, not read your Bible, not have a prayer life, and not be consistent, you are simply a sitting duck for the enemy of your soul. Those who have been around for a while are no better off. If we could only see the demonic forces and the satanic faces behind each temptation, we would understand what Paul said in II Timothy 2:22, *"Flee also youthful lusts."* We would run like a wild man away from it. It would look like the worst horror show Hollywood could produce times ten if we could see the real face of Satan behind every temptation we face.

Speaking of the fool who goes after the harlot, the Bible says in Proverbs 9:18, *"But he knoweth not that the dead are there; and that her guests are in the depths of hell."* Proverbs 2:18 says, *"For her house inclineth unto death, and her paths unto the dead. None that go unto her return again, neither take they hold of the paths of life."* When I read that I almost get the impression that God is saying that men never recover from adultery. While there is grace, the Bible says that none that go unto her ever return again. Maybe that is what the Bible means when it says in Proverbs 6:32, *"But whoso committeth adultery with a woman lacketh understanding: he that doeth it destroyeth his own soul."* The soul is where decisions are made. It is also the seat of your will and emotions. Some of the skyrocketing suicide rates we see among God's people may be because somebody has raped their soul of its innocence. No matter how hard they pray to get right with God, they cannot seem to rid their minds of the demonic images.

2. He Often Uses Earthly Foes.

In Genesis 3:1 he is *"the serpent"* and in I Peter 5:8 he *"walketh about... as a roaring lion."* The key word in this verse is *"as."* The devil wants you to think he is one thing when, in fact, he is another. Satan is the only creation of God who wants absolutely no credit for anything he does. He disguises himself to deceive us.

A. He Can Appear As An Angel Of Light.

II Corinthians 11:13 says, *"Satan himself is transformed into an angel of light."* He will do everything he can to make you think that he is not in the sin.

> **Satan is the only creation of God who wants absolutely no credit for what he does.**

B. He Can Appear As A Friend To A Young Person.

Every young person that has ever lived has faced the temptation at some time in his life to be drawn away from his parents. It does not matter if it is a sincere friend that looks good; you need to run as fast as you can. You are right now in the presence of evil because they are drawing you away from that which God put in your life to protect you.

He can deceive you into thinking you are above accountability. Men, God gave you a wife. Although you are the leader in your home, leadership does not give you the right to live above accountability. I want my wife to know where I am all the time because I do not want to be in the wrong place. Being accountable to someone helps me to stay careful. I have my Bible reading calendar in the front of my Bible for my wife to see. I do not flaunt it, but I make sure she sees it every once in awhile because I want her to know I am not a fraud or a windbag. I wonder how many of our precious wives live in fear every day of whether or not their husbands are living right because he will not be accountable to anybody.

Although we believe in a pastor-led church, that does not mean the pastor is above accountability. While I am not accountable to *any one* person *individually*; I am accountable to *every* person in my church *collectively*. My church has every right to know what I do with my time. People that think their time is nobody's business are just wrong. As long as we live in this fallen world, being free from accountability makes you an Adolph Hitler. In the New Testament Church Age we are supposed to be *servants*, not *sovereigns; ministers*, not *monarchs*.

At the Battle of Gettysburg, a general reported to General Longstreet that it was impossible to bring his men up to the fight again. Longstreet sarcastically responded, "Very well, then, never mind. Just let them stay where they are. The enemy is going to advance, and that will spare you the trouble." That is where many of us are. We say, "I just can't do it," but then you do not have to; the devil will come to you. I would like to take the fight to him instead of him bringing the fight to me. If I will take the fight to him, I can determine the battle plan instead of his always setting me up.

> ***Leadership does not give you the right to live above accountability.***

You better recognize your foe! We are in a fight for our lives, our souls, our families! We are in a fight for our faith! There are a lot of folks in America who do not like us – not just the heathen, but even other Christians and Baptists. Would to God that independent, fundamental Baptists would get as fired up as queers are. Matthew 22:18 says, *"But Jesus perceived their wickedness, and said, Why tempt ye me, ye hypocrites?"* Luke 10:25: *"And, behold, a certain lawyer stood up, and tempted him..."* Over and over again, the Bible says that Jesus understood that the hypocrite and the lawyer were simply tools being used by His real enemy – the devil.

We Must Resolve To Fight

1. *We Must Enjoy Victory*

Ephesians 6:12 says, *"For we wrestle not against flesh and blood, but against principalities, against powers, against the rulers of the darkness of this world, against spiritual wickedness in high places."* I love the word *wrestle*. It means, "to struggle, to be involved in a battle." Some of you need to get with it. We all lose every once in awhile, but at least put up a fight! Let the devil know that when he is done with you, although you may be bloody or have an ear ripped off, you make sure that he is limping away, too. I knew that as soon as I shared this study with anyone the devil would say, "Aha, we're going to see about Jon Jenkins. We're going to see if he can handle what he's preaching." The devil has not left me alone; he knows I am messing with his world. I am not the master of the devil, but my Saviour is. As long as I am right with Him, the two of us can get the job done!

I preach a lot of my convictions, and even a few of my preferences, because I am trying to let the devil know that I want to fight. I am not just going to play dead. In the last ten to twenty years, I have seen independent Baptist churches all over the country stop preaching on standards, convictions, and

> *This is a ferocious fight that we must engage in valiantly if we hope to enjoy the victory!*

page • 56

holy living. They say, "Well, all that did was raise up trouble and offend people. We're just going to talk about love now." They are really saying, "Devil, just do what you want. We aren't going to mess with you anymore."

2. We Must Engage Valiantly

A. In The Right Places

In Matthew 4:1 Jesus was led into the wilderness to be tempted of the devil. That word *wilderness* implies "barrenness." Think about where the first Adam was tempted and where the second Adam was tempted. The first Adam encountered Satan in a garden, lost the battle, and was sent into the wilderness. The second Adam encountered Satan in a wilderness, won the battle, and faced him again in a garden. Jesus had just ended thirty years of being the best boy any momma ever had. When he walked into the last three-year phase of His life in His earthly ministry, He was led into the wilderness and ran into the same foe Adam met, but Jesus resisted him the entire time. Every time the devil tried to quote Scripture, Jesus said, "Nope, I have another Scripture for that." By the time He was done quoting Scripture, He said, "Devil, get away from me!"

The devil came back to see Him three years later in a garden. The devil tried to get the Lord to quit, and he got Him close. Somehow Jesus said, "No, I am not going to give in. I am going to trust the Bible. I am going to trust my Father." He said, *"O my Father, if it be possible, let this cup pass from me: nevertheless not as I will, but as thou wilt."* The *living* Word of God found the strength from the *written* Word of God. The first Adam lost the battle in a garden and was put in the wilderness. The second Adam met the devil in the wilderness and ended up getting the victory in the garden. The second Adam absolutely reversed everything the first Adam lost, and it was in a garden tomb that he rose up out of the grave and walked away.

> *Following Satan's seductions will always lead you to a place of barrenness, but following the Saviour's steps will always lead you to a place of blessing.*

Following Satan's Seduction will always lead you to a place of ***Barrenness***, but ***Following the Savior's Steps*** will always lead you to a place of ***Blessings***.

B. With The Right Prayer

John 16:33 says, *"These things I have spoken unto you, that in me ye might have peace. In the world ye shall have tribulation: but be of good cheer; I have overcome the world."* Jesus said, "Follow me out of the barrenness of the wilderness and into the garden of blessing." Our biggest problem is that we start too many of our days following our*selves* instead of following *Him*. How dare we spend twenty-four hours without checking in at headquarters to find out our battle plan? No wonder the devil messes us up, trips us up, and twists us up. We do not even know *where* we are let alone *who* we are.

C. With The Right Perspective

When you look at Jon Jenkins, you see a fallen, human, weak, wayward, straying, prone-to-wander man. But that is not what the Lord sees. He sees a soldier, a warrior. He says, *"Nay, in all these things we are more than conquerors through him that loved us,"* (Romans 8:37) and *"Greater is he that is in you, than he that is in the world"* (I John 4:4). The devil wants you to see yourself the way *you* see yourself, not the way *God* sees you. He does not want you to realize that you are a warrior. That is why we dress warriors up. When the Marines from our church are home with their uniforms on, they are a little cocky. They have their chests out a little bit. The Marines dress their boys that way because that is exactly how they want them to act. I do not know if the Marines are the best, but they dead sure *think* they are. I do not know if they can whip more people than the army can, but they *think* they can. I am afraid that some of us have spent so long looking like losers and deadbeats that we do not understand that we are soldiers in the army of God! We need to walk like it, act like it, and talk like it! You might be surprised – the devil might run a little more from you. He runs *to* us because he is not expecting much resistance.

In John Hunter's book *Knowing God's Secrets*, he tells how that as a young believer seeking to live for God, he was much distressed by the problem of temptation. He imagined that as he grew older he would assume a tangible form of respectability which would solve the problem of temptation and that he would eventually arrive at the state where he would be free from temptation's awful effects. As the years passed, he realized that he had been deceived and stated he had learned two basic realities:

- *Temptation is just as strong and subtle in mature Christians as in young Christians.*
- *Mature Christians are just as weak and prone to fall as young Christians.*

That means that you have to keep fighting if you are planning on winning.

D. With The Right Perseverance

Many who are my age in the Lord have the danger of thinking we have it all figured out. The devil has been doing his work for 6,000 years. Even if you are old, you have not even lived one day in his economy and are no match for the devil. You will never live long enough to be a match for the devil. He takes more out in one day than you and I will face in temptations in a lifetime. The only way he can be dealt with is in a **warrior mode**. The older we get, the more we want to relax. We say, "I used to be a bus worker. I used to serve in the Sunday school. I used to work in those children's church services. Now I'm old, and I've done my job. Let those young kids do all the work." Then the devil says, "Ha, ha, ha. I've been waiting for the day to ruin him." Some of you need to get ugly. Instead of saying "I used to", say I'm going to start *doing* again!" Get back in the fight!

We Must Resist With Faith

Ephesians 6:16 says, *"…Above all, taking the shield of faith, wherewith ye shall be able to quench all the fiery darts of the wicked."* Let's look at when and why Jesus was tempted that we may seize the victory over temptation.

1. Jesus Was Tempted *After* His Obedience.

Mark 1:9-12 says, *"Jesus came from Nazareth of Galilee, and was baptized of John in Jordan… And immediately the Spirit driveth him into the wilderness."* I would rather be surrendered and fight a battle, than to be disobedient and rebellious and have the devil not even consider me a serious enough threat to mess with. The fact that you never play in the game is not a good thing. If I am going to football training camp in August, drill two practices a day, and run my guts out; I do not want to sit on the bench. You only get messed up, knocked around, and bloodied, when you are either running with the ball or blocking for the guy running the ball. When it is game time, it is so much more fun to be in the game than on the bench.

So many of God's people are content to sit on the bench and hope the devil won't go after them. However, why are you content to be a bench warmer to keep the devil from giving you any opposition? It may sound crazy, but I like to play in the game. I want him to know that I am going a different direction than he is. I want him to know that I am opposing him – that what he is doing is different than what I am doing.

Jesus' temptation followed His baptism. Remember the old adage, "He who most closely follows the Saviour will be most closely followed by Satan." You may say, "Preacher, it seems like the more I have surrendered to God, the worse things are getting." No, you are more in the will of God than you have ever been in your life; and the proof of that is how much the devil is opposing you. In Mark 1:10-11, when Jesus obediently followed in baptism, **Heaven's Spirit Bestowed A Holy Anointing** – *"the Spirit like a dove descending upon him,"* and also **Heaven's Sovereign Bequeathed A Heavenly Approval** – *"Thou art my beloved Son, in whom I am well pleased."* It is only to be expected that **The Anointing Will Be Assaulted**.

> *He who most closely follows the Saviour will be most closely followed by Satan.*

You may not want the devil fighting you, but you should be pleased with the fact that he is fighting you. It means that he recognizes an anointing and an approval on your life. Do you ever think about the fact that a thief never robs poor people? Why don't the robbers go to trailer parks? They go to the big fancy houses – ones owned by doctors and executives. The highway robber watches for the man with plenty. The devil wants to rob you of your riches. The fact that he is assaulting you means that he knows you have something. These riches are why you ought to fight harder than you have ever fought in your life.

Every dad knows what I am talking about. God gives you

a precious little baby girl or boy, and you feel protective. You feel that way because you realize that God has given you such a precious treasure.

If the old devil comes by my way tomorrow and decides that he is going to mess me up, he is going to have to understand that he is talking about one of God's boys. I read about the day he knocked the devil's teeth out, stole his keys from him, put His foot on his neck and said, "Death and hell are done!" I am not proud of me, but I am proud of my Daddy! And I am hid in Him! Every time the devil messes with me, he is messing with my Daddy. Quit acting like a *Victim* and start acting like a *Victor*. When the devil knocks you down say, "The reason you knocked me down is because you know I am going to get back up!" The *Foe Opposes* whom the *Father Approves.*

2. Jesus Was Tempted <u>Before</u> His Opportunity.

Jesus was tempted *after His obedience* and *before His opportunity*. Mark 1:13-14: *"And he was there in the wilderness forty days, tempted of Satan… Now after that John was put in prison, Jesus came into Galilee, preaching the gospel of the kingdom of God."* The devil is messing with you so bad because He knows what God is about to do with you, and he would like to disqualify you before God uses you.

Look at the three temptations with which Satan tempted Jesus:

Temptation #1: Disobedience, With His Body, Which Is Physical

Matthew 4:3-4 says, *"And when the tempter came to him, he said, If thou be the Son of God, command that these stones be made bread."* Having just fasted forty days, Jesus was hungry. His response to Satan's temptation was, *"Man shall not live by bread alone, but by every word that proceedeth out of the mouth of God."* Satan appealed to Jesus' physical need. The devil was trying to get him to eat when He knew that if He would just trust God, God would take care of Him. He is the *Bread of Life* – He does not need anything from the devil! If you are saved, you have the *Bread of Life* available to you. Why are you eating at the devil's table?

Temptation #2: Pride, With His Soul, Which Is Emotional

Matthew 4:5-7 states, *"Then the devil taketh him up into the holy city, and setteth him on a pinnacle of the temple, And saith unto him, If thou be the Son of God, cast thyself down: for it is written, He shall give his angels charge concerning thee: and in their hands they shall bear thee up, lest at any time thou dash thy foot against a stone."* Jesus said, *"Thou shalt not tempt the Lord thy God."* That temptation was a temptation to His soul – an emotional temptation. He is trying to appeal to Jesus' pride. He tried to get Jesus to be presumptuous and hurt Himself intentionally just to prove He was God. The devil wanted Him to be prideful.

Temptation #3: Worshipping Satan, With His Spirit, Which Is Spiritual.

Matthew 4:8-11 tells us, *"Again, the devil taketh him up into an exceeding high mountain, and sheweth him all the kingdoms of the world, and the glory of them; And saith unto him, All these things will I give thee, if thou wilt fall down and worship me. Then saith Jesus unto him, Get thee hence, Satan: for it is written, Thou shalt worship the Lord thy God, and him only shalt thou serve. Then the devil leaveth him, and, behold, angels came and ministered unto him."* Child of God, Jesus faced every kind of temptation man can face – emotional, spiritual, and physical – and He walked away from all three of them victorious. He had His eye on the opportunities that were before Him. What lay *before* Christ troubled the devil more than what lay *behind* Him! *"Looking unto Jesus…who for the joy that was set before him endured the cross, despising the shame"* (Hebrews 12:2). As much of a mess as the devil has made of your life, what is in front of you bothers him more than what is behind you.

The devil figured that if by any means he could disqualify the One who was capable of doing so much damage to his kingdom he might be able to put off being defeated at the cross. Jesus faced such a foe because the devil knew the future. The devil knew that if Jesus ever got free of his temptation his day was over. Just like Jesus, the devil comes to you because he knows that you are about to make an absolute showing of God's power in your life. And just like Jesus, you can have victory over the presence of evil behind the temptation.

To summarize all of this, we see that:

TEMPTATION IS PROVIDENTIAL

Temptation is not always a bad thing to face. The devil was the tempter, but he was not the leader in Jesus' story. Jesus was led by the *Spirit* into the wilderness to be tempted. That is why Jesus said, *"When ye pray, say, . . . Lead us not into temptation"* (Luke 11:1-4). Some days God *does* lead you into temptation. He does not tempt you with evil, but He leads you there because He has a purpose in mind to show you what you are made of. He may want to reveal to you exactly how spiritual you are or what exactly you are trusting in.

TEMPTATION IS PERSONAL

I have had men ask me many times, "Preacher, do you think I should get rid of Internet at my house?" Let me ask *you* a question, "How are you doing with the temptation, sir?" If you are not licking it, and it is licking you, the answer is absolutely, unequivocally, "Yes!" I am not sure that we can make the argument that it is wicked for every Christian to have the Internet, but it is wicked for *you* if you cannot handle it. There are things that the devil could throw at me that would not faze me, but if he threw them at you, you would fall flat on your face. There are some things that he throws at you that do not even faze you, but if he threw them at me, I would trip so fast that I would not even know I was walking to begin with.

In speaking of convictions, the Bible says, *"Let every man be fully persuaded in his own mind"* (Romans 14:5b). Do you know where you are weak? If you are weak somewhere, then stop spending time letting that stuff into your life. We are not to make provisions for our flesh. Notice that it does not say provision for *other people's* flesh but for your *own* flesh. If you do not know where you are weak, you will spend your Christian life falling and stumbling in the dark. I know where I am weak. I discover every day someplace that I am weaker, but I generally know where I am weak. That is why I have some of the convictions I have. As one old preacher said, "I don't have all these Bible convictions because I am spiritual – I have them because I am **not** spiritual." We do not want you to do certain things because we do not want you to mess up your life.

Temptation Is a Proving

By defeating the devil, Jesus proved His worthiness to be our God and High Priest. *"For we have not an high priest which cannot be touched with the feeling of our infirmities; but was in all points tempted like as we are, yet without sin"* (Hebrews 4:15). He was already God, but He was God and man. He was the God-man. Every temptation He faced in that hour in the wilderness was not in the power of deity but in the power of humanity. If He had whipped the devil in His own deity, you and I would have no recourse to follow His example. For forty days, Jesus put Himself where we live to prove to us that the devil can be defeated by someone who has his eye on the goal, not on what is going on just this moment. By ***Conquering***, He proved His ***Competence***!

A servant of God is proven by temptation. We prove a bridge by putting weight upon it, and we prove the quality of gold by putting it in the fire. Temptations in our life are often times God wants to prove whether or not the bridge He has built can handle the weight. Jesus proved that He was the conqueror by the way He handled his forty days in the wilderness. The great reformer Martin Luther once said, "I would never have been the man that I am were it not for the devil." The devil was needed in his life to prove that he was really what he claimed to be. As long as you are in the flesh, you will not win every temptation; however, it should bother you that you do not win very many. If you fall time and time and time again, you either do not give a flip, or you need to see if you know God.

> *"I would never have been the man that I am were it not for the devil."*
>
> ~ Martin Luther

I wish I could tell you that I have won the victory in every area – God knows I wish I could say that; but I can look into my trophy case and see I have *some* trophies. I have won *some* ground. I have won *some* battles. Child of God, every time you win a battle, God is proving to you that He has more for you to do – bigger opportunities and greater days ahead. Do not let the devil rob you of being used of God by tripping you up over the same stupid root.

Had Jesus failed in His hour of temptation, He would have

failed in every other area of His life. That is why the Spirit led Him into the wilderness: To prove to the world that He was the real thing.

Temptation Is Painful

My wife and I were in San Diego walking along the beach when I saw thirty men a mile off shore swimming. It was wintertime. The Pacific Ocean is not warm that time of year. We came back another day, later in the day, and those men were swimming again. I asked Brother Doug Fisher of Lighthouse Baptist Church in San Diego, California, what those men were doing. He said, "Oh, that is the Navy Seals training. They are swimming ten miles every day in the surf in freezing cold water. That is why there are only a few hundred Navy Seals in the entire world." We do not need a lot of men; we just need the BEST men.

When God is training warriors, He will not put you in the wading pool where the water is warm and the little kiddies splash around. God said, "You want to be a great evangelist, young man, you want to be a great missionary, you want to be a great servant of God, you want to be a preacher's wife, you want to stand beside a man of God and help him dent the kingdom of darkness, then welcome into the ocean! I know it is January, but welcome in anytime!"

College days will always be tough because the devil knows the opportunities. I know that it is not God's will for every student who starts Bible college to finish, but it breaks my heart when I see students leave school because of things that I faced in my own college days but for which I got on my knees and found God. I am not mad at them. Some quit because they did not have what it took. They were good people. When I was in college, I saw hundreds quit. Some of them are in churches today serving God; they were good people. I am not saying that a layman is less than a preacher. However, whatever God's opportunity is for you, He will train you accordingly.

Temptation Is Pressure

If I was hired to drive a truck, I could impress the boss all day long pulling a trailer as long as I did not have to back up. I could impress the boss without much training going straight down the road with no curves, good weather, and no cars on the road. But if the boss were to put me in a truck with $100,000 worth of equipment when there was ten inches of snow falling, he would want to make sure I knew what I was doing. He would want to make sure that his truck would not be part of a pile-up in front of me. He would probably ride with me a few days and scold me and get after me. How are you doing with your battle in temptation?

Harry Truman was a good president, but he was not popular. Truman was underestimated the entire time he was president. I am glad that he was the one in office at the end of World War II. I love the Japanese people, but there was a different spirit in the world back then. We were at war, and we had an enemy. There were some calculations that one million Americans might die in the attack on Japan's mainland. The President said, *"My number one job is not to please the world but to protect my nation. The safest thing for my country is to try to end this war as quickly as I can."* He dropped the atomic bomb. I do not know if the Japanese quite knew what hit them, but they knew the second time. They knew from then on that they were dealing with one tough man in the White House. They gave up. Harry Truman meant what he said, and what he said was exactly what was going to happen. Harry Truman was a straight shooter from the heartland of our country.

According to Harry Truman's biographer, David McCullough, President Truman was under incredible pressure while attending the Potsdam Conference. It was a very tough conference also attended by Churchill and Stalin. Truman was new on the stage. They had been dealing with Franklin Roosevelt for a long time. Churchill and Stalin both underestimated Harry Truman. He put a lot of energy into that conference as they were talking about how they were going to divide Europe after World War II. He was lonely, tired, and physically exhausted. One evening, near the end of an arduous session at the palace, as Truman's limousine was taking him to his hotel, they picked up a young Army public relations officer who was hitchhiking.

The young man was so excited about being with the President that he said, "Sir, I know Berlin well. Is there anything that you need or want? I can get it for you. The black market in this city is rampant. I can get you booze, cigarettes, watches, whiskey, or even women if you want."

The President said, "What did you say? I am married to my sweetheart, and my sweetheart is married to me. My wife doesn't cheat on me, and I don't cheat on my wife. Chauffeur, stop the car and let this boy walk home."

When it was all done, the chauffeur thought that it was a rude response, but Harry Truman never missed a beat. He acted like it never happened. He went home that night and slept alone in his bed. Harry Truman proved himself that night. Nobody would have known, but before God allowed him to be president in such a dark hour, He had already tested the weight of the bridge. God is not going to put you in a place where you will destroy your testimony. He has us where we are right now and allows the devil to tempt us every once in awhile to see if we are ready for a greater day and a greater place of service for Jesus Christ. You had better understand that when the devil is there, not only what you are facing right now is at stake, but *everything* is at stake.

3

Praying Earnestly

Prayer provides the strength to resist temptation.

Watch and pray, that ye enter not into temptation: the spirit indeed is willing, but the flesh is weak. **Matthew 26:41**

And said unto them, Why sleep ye? rise and pray, lest ye enter into temptation. **Luke 22:46**

After reviewing the verses above that speak plainly on the matter of prayer, it is safe to assume that:

1. We should pray that God would not lead us into temptation.
2. It is true that prayer can give us victory from temptation.
3. The reason that prayer plays such an important role in temptation is that the flesh is weak in all of us.

By God's grace, we are beginning to discover some details about this danger of temptation. However, I want to warn you not to think so foolishly as to assume that you now have temptation figured out. It is often just after we gain a little victory that we suffer our greatest defeat! In teaching on this subject, I have made the devil mad. That has convinced me that this is an important subject. It has also convinced me that we should be careful not to think we have temptation figured out and stop being careful.

I am reminded of a story about a soldier who shouted to his comrades through the darkness,

"I caught a prisoner!"

His commanding officer shouted back, "Bring him in!"

He answered, "He won't come."

The officer said, "Then you come yourself!"

The reply came, "He won't let me!"

I fear too many of us think we are victors when, in truth, we are still captives. In all of my study for this book, I discovered almost nothing in print about the angle on temptation I am taking here. I have heard little preaching that goes in the direction of this chapter. This is virgin territory in the subject of temptation.

Jesus Used The Bible To Defeat Temptation

The Bible records the Savior's reaction of each temptation the devil threw at Him in the wilderness. He responded to each temptation with the words, *"It is written!"* He would not let the devil get Him to depart from the Bible. He stuck with the Bible, and that tells me that the Word of God was His *Resource* that was the secret to His triumph! If you do not get this figured out, you will not defeat temptation. You might decide to just try harder, but your willpower will never be a big enough match for the devil.

I am going to surprise you with this statement: The more you try to defeat the devil in your own willpower, the more you are strengthening your old nature. The stronger your flesh is, the weaker you become. If we are not supposed to try harder, then what is the secret to victory? It is as simple as the B-I-B-L-E! If

> *The Word of God was the resource that was the secret to Jesus' triumph over temptation!*

you do not read the Bible, quit talking about trying to win the victory over temptation. Pastor Marvin Smith of Harvest Baptist Church in Fort Dodge, Iowa, said at our camp meeting in 2004, "In the pornography-soaked, licentious culture we are living in today, no good Christian man is going to stay spiritual reading less than ten chapters of the Bible a day."

I have read through my Bible for years now, but that statement by Brother Smith put me under deep conviction. Ten chapters a day means that I would get through my Bible about three and a half times a year. Brother Smith, an authority on spiritual warfare, said very plainly that no Christian man is going to be spiritual and stay on top in the world in which we are living on less than ten chapters of Bible per day. Are you even getting in one chapter a day? Do you allow three or four days to go by without even touching your Bible? Someone has said, "Seven days without the Bible makes one weak." The Word of God is a weapon we use in spiritual warfare. When you open your Bible each morning to read and meditate and pray, you are engaged in spiritual warfare. When you start a day and never open the

Bible, you are declaring to the devil, his demons, and the dear Lamb of God, "I don't need God today. I can handle these guys by myself!" That method does not work. The devil will have you twisted in knots before noon!

Now, the Word of God was Jesus' *Resource* for His triumph. If *Jesus* needed the Word of God, what is *our* hope without it? If the *Living Word* of God had to have the *Written* Word of God as His resource to be successful in His battle with temptation, then why are you and I trying to mess with the devil without getting in the Bible every single day?

My wife was speaking at a ladies' meeting when a well-respected man of God's wife walked up to her and said, "Debbie, I am embarrassed to tell you that I don't even read my Bible every day." This was a preacher's wife. Do you read your Bible every day? I do not mean just two or three verses, I mean read your Bible to get armed for the day of battle. You are involved in spiritual warfare whether you read your Bible or not, but success is impossible without reading it.

Let me communicate to you ladies. If you are in your thirties and are having trouble with your emotions, you have not seen anything yet! Something is coming in your life called menopause. You will embark on a level of insecurity and instability you have never before experienced. It might last for a few weeks or a few days, but it might last for the rest of your life! I am not trying to hurt or offend anyone, but I have observed over the years that ladies who are self-willed have a worse time in menopause than any other group of ladies because self-willed ladies did not need God enough when they were strong.

Precious lady, when God said that He made you the weaker vessel, He was referring to your emotions. He made you to be vulnerable. Ladies and men alike need to walk with God. Men's and ladies' battles differ in that men battle more in the area of the thought life while women battle more in the area of emotions. Many a wife manipulates her husband because she is full of confusion. Instead of manipulating your husband, use your Weapon and win some battles in spiritual warfare.

The Word of God was Jesus' *Resource* for His triumph, but what was His *Source* or His power for His triumph? From where did the power come to resist? From where did the power come for Him to say, "Devil, it is written"? From hearing the temptation to saying "*it is written*," He faced the same battle in His flesh that you face, and He licked the devil. Where did He get the power?

JESUS USED PRAYER TO DEFEAT TEMPTATION

Remember when Mary and Joseph unknowingly left Jesus in the temple? They had taken him at twelve years of age to the annual feast. On the way home, they supposed He was in their company but could not find Him. When they returned to Jerusalem, they found Him in the house of God. He was sitting in the temple with the great learned men of the law. The rabbis were sitting around dumbfounded that He was answering questions that they could not answer.

His momma walked in and said, "Son, we have been looking

for you. We didn't know where to find you." He looked at His momma and said, "Momma, why did you have trouble finding me? You knew where I would have been. 'I must be about my Father's business' (Luke 2:49)." When He was twelve years of age, He had already begun to understand that He had a plan and a goal for His life that was unlike anyone else's. A little later in His earthly ministry, He walked into that same temple He had been in as a boy and said, "*My house is the house of prayer*" (Luke 19:46).

In the early hours of His earthly ministry, He declared that His Father's house was a house of prayer. I believe in preaching, but He did not call it a house of preaching. I believe in worship and praise, but He did not call it a house of worship and praise. I believe in sacrifices and offerings and giving, but He did not call it a house of sacrifices and offerings and giving. He called the house of God, His Father's house where He must be about His business, a house of prayer.

When Jesus arrived in Bethany after Lazarus had died, Martha was mad at Him, rebuking Him for not getting there sooner. Mary was so depressed and discouraged that she did not even come to meet Him. Right before He told Lazarus to come forth, He stopped and said something to God so everyone else could hear it. He said, "*Father, I thank thee that thou hast heard me. And I knew that thou hearest me always: but because of the people which stand by I said it, that they may believe that thou hast sent me*" (John 11:41-42).

At twelve years of age, He said, "I must be about my Father's business." As he began His earthly ministry and threw the money changers out of the temple, He called His Father's house a house of prayer. In John 11 when He raised His dear friend Lazarus from the grave, He made a declaration so all could hear, "Every time I pray, my Father hears and answers my prayer." When He said, "*I knew that thou hearest me always,*" they were not the words of an insincere hypocrite. They were words of One who had obviously spent much time in that sweet hour of prayer.

Is it any wonder that the Bible says in Mark 1:35, "*And in the morning, rising up a great while before day, he went out, and departed into a solitary place, and there prayed.*" Is it any wonder that Mark 6:46 says, "*And when he had sent them away, he departed into a mountain to pray.*" Is it any wonder that Luke 6:12 says, "*And it came to pass in those days, that he went out into a mountain to pray, and continued all night in prayer to God.*" It is clear that the greatest prayer warrior in the Bible was not the Apostle Paul. It was not the Apostle Peter. It was not Martha or Mary or Mary Magdalene. The greatest prayer warrior in the Bible was Jesus.

I hope I have made the point that prayer was an intricate part of Jesus' life and ministry. When His disciples were about ready to face a temptation bigger than anything they had yet faced, He made a statement that He had learned very well in His own experience. "*Watch and pray, that ye enter not into temptation.*" I am going to make three statements about temptation and prayer.

We Must Understand The Exhortation

And he cometh unto the disciples, and findeth them asleep, and saith unto Peter, What, could ye not watch with me one hour? ***Watch and pray,*** *that ye enter not into temptation: the spirit indeed is willing, but the flesh is weak.*
Matthew 26:40-41

Watch ye and pray, *lest ye enter into temptation. The spirit truly is ready, but the flesh is weak.* **Mark 14:38**

And said unto them, Why sleep ye? ***rise and pray,*** *lest ye enter into temptation.* **Luke 22:4**

In all three places, He says "ye." Jesus declared that we must *watch and pray* and that we must *rise and pray*, lest we enter into temptation. He was saying that you either fall *in supplication* or fall *to temptation*. I have had hundreds of people in over twenty years of being a man of God sit across my desk and tell me that there is some area in their life in which they have struggled and fallen. I have never had one person out of several hundred say, "Now, preacher, I want to make something clear, though. When I fell, when I yielded, when I gave in, when I crossed the line, my prayer life was in the best shape it had ever been." What I **have** heard, even from preachers in the ministry is, "Preacher, for about six months (or two years) before I fell, my prayer life dried up."

I sat across the table from a man recently that is in an absolute disastrous situation because of sin in his life. He said, "Preacher, the amazing thing about what I have been through is that I have been reading my Bible faithfully. I have not missed reading my Bible." But

> *You either Fall*
> *In Supplication*
> *or you Fall*
> *To Temptation.*

then big tears began to flow down his cheeks as he said, "But, oh, my prayer life. Preacher, I have never had a prayer life. I pray occasionally and even get fired up in revival meetings, but I have never had a prayer list or prayed for an hour or even half an hour."

There is something to numerology in the Bible. I preached a message years ago entitled, "The Trinity and the Resurrection" and showed many of the trinities in the Bible. There were three inner disciples (Peter, James, and John), three crosses (Jesus and the two thieves), three members of the Godhead (Father, Son, and Holy Spirit), three parts of our being (body, soul, and spirit), three parts to the family (father, mother, and children), three branches of our government (legislative, executive, and judicial), and three parts to the Bible (Old Testament, Inter-Testament, and New Testament). Salvation is a trinity (justification, sanctification, and glorification). The universe is a trinity (space, matter, and time). All three parts of the universe are also a trinity. Space is a trinity (identified in the first dimension, seen in the second dimension, and experienced in the third dimension). The mathematical equation of space is 1 x 1 x 1=1, not 1 + 1 + 1=3, just like God. Matter is a trinity (generated in energy, seen through motion, and experienced by phenomena). Time is a trinity (past, present, and future). The elements are a trinity (solid, liquid, and vapor). Directions are a trinity (north and south, east and west, up and down). The Gospel is a trinity (death, burial, and resurrection of Christ). Jesus, according to John 14:6, is a trinity (the way, the truth, and the life).

Even the most basic building block of life is a trinity. Atoms have three parts – protons, neutrons, and electrons. I could keep going. The reason is because God made nature in His own image, and God is a trinity. Each part of nature – matter, time, and energy – is also broken down into three parts. I preached that message because there was a first resurrection, a second resurrection, and there is a third one coming! As sure as God and nature are trinities, even so the resurrection is a trinity. Jesus is coming again!

I want to tell you about another trinity. Three times in His temptation, Jesus said, *"It is written."* Three times in the Bible He makes that statement, *"Watch and pray lest ye enter into temptation!"* In Matthew 26:39-44 we see another trinity connected to the principle of how closely related temptation and prayer really are. Remember that Jesus was tempted three times in His earthly ministry. His final temptation is shown to us in Matthew 26.

Jesus was in the Garden of Gethsemane, and the devil had Him closer than ever to quitting, unraveling, and undoing the entire plan of redemption. Matthew 26:39 says, *"And he went a little further, and fell on his face, and prayed, saying, O my*

Father, if it be possible, let this cup pass from me: nevertheless not as I will, but as thou wilt." Jesus was facing the temptation to quit. If He had, you would be on your way to hell right now. The Bible says that Jesus did not have the strength to face His cup, yet He still had the strength to say, *"Father, not as I will, but as Thou wilt."*

And he cometh unto the disciples, and findeth them asleep, and saith unto Peter, What, could ye not watch with me one hour? Watch and pray, that ye enter not into temptation: the spirit indeed is willing, but the flesh is weak. He went away again the second time, and prayed, saying, O my Father, if this cup may not pass away from me, except I drink it, thy will be done. And he came and found them asleep again: for their eyes were heavy. And he left them, and went away again, and prayed the third time, saying the same words. **Matthew 26:40-44**

Judas was leading the servants and officers of the high priest to the garden as this prayer meeting began. You do not know what the forces of evil are already plotting to do in your life. Ephesians 6 talks of an *"evil day."* This was Jesus' evil day. He did not pray one or two times; he prayed three times. Three times He said, *"It is written."* Three times He said, *"Watch and pray, lest ye enter into temptation."* Three times in His last temptation, He went and received energy.

The children's song goes, *"Read your Bible, pray every day, and you'll grow, grow, grow."* Isn't that what we teach the boys and girls? Are *you* growing?   You may think you are just struggling, but you are not just "struggling." You are not reading your Bible or praying. The Word of God was important in Jesus' temptation, but the Bible was only part of the answer. The Bible and prayer are of equal importance.

The big problem in our Christian lives is that we have a hard time staying balanced. We get in ditches. We get zealous for soul winning and lay out of our Bible reading. Then we get all fired up for Bible reading and lay out of our prayer life. The Bible says in Proverbs 11:1, *"A false balance is abomination to the LORD: but a just weight is his delight."* God wants you and I to have balance. Regrettably, the average Christian thinks that balance is an equal amount of worldliness and godliness in his life. That combination equals them out to be nothing. If you are a forty-five minute Bible reader, then you need to be a forty-five minute prayer. If you are an hour Bible reader, then you need to be an hour prayer. You will not lick the devil until you understand the **Power of the Scriptures** and the **Power of Supplication.**

John Wycliffe once said, "Let no man think himself to be holy because he is not tempted, for the holiest and highest in life have the most temptations. How much higher the hill is, so much is the wind there greater; so, how much higher the life is, so much the stronger is the temptation of the enemy."

It is not your standing but your kneeling that delivers you from the power of darkness! It does not matter if you are a Sunday school teacher or the pastor of a church. It does not matter if you are a child or a deacon. It does not matter what your standing is. Your battle with temptation is not about where you stand but rather where you kneel.

When missionary Praying (John) Hyde died, they went to his little prayer chamber on the side of his home and began to sort through his study. They were dumbfounded when they found, in a little corner, two grooves in the oak floor over an inch deep. On the wall in front of those grooves was a dark spot. At first they could not tell what the spot was, but they finally analyzed that it was his breath stain. He had worn grooves in the floor where he had interceded for his friends, loved ones, and world. He had left a stained board on a wall where he had prayed for hours on end.

The average American's Christianity is 3,000 miles wide and one inch deep. In China, the Christianity is about one inch wide and 3,000 miles deep. A. W. Tozer was a Christian Missionary Alliance preacher. He was probably most famous because he produced the *Alliance Weekly*. He wrote fifty books in his lifetime, some of the greatest books ever written. The book of his that I love the most is entitled *In Pursuit of God*. He pastored a great church; edited a weekly, national publication; and wrote fifty books. He wrote some of the greatest literature I have ever read in my life that will put you under conviction like you never imagined. A. W. Tozer's biographer said that it was not unusual for him to pray six hours a day.

> *It is not your Standing, but your Kneeling, that delivers you from the power of darkness.*

When Dr. Tom Malone was a young preacher in his

thirties and had just left evangelism to start a church in Pontiac, Michigan, he was asked by the Grace Theological Seminary of Winona Lake, Indiana, to preach for a week to the preacher boys on being filled with the Holy Spirit. The young preacher was honored beyond description, especially when he found out that he was to preach with A. W. Tozer. He was scared to be preaching with the great legend. The morning after the first night of services at Winona Lake, Dr. Malone and Dr. Tozer were eating breakfast together.

Dr. Malone said, "Dr. Tozer, I have to ask you a question. I know why you're here, but I have no idea why I have been asked to speak here this week. Brother Tozer, I am not even sure if I am filled with the Spirit of God, and that is our subject. Please tell me how to be filled with the Holy Ghost."

Dr. Tozer pushed his bowl of oatmeal away, and they began to talk about the fullness of the Holy Spirit. Dr. Tozer quoted John 5:35, *"He was a burning and a shining light."* He said, "Tom, do you want to shine, or do you want to burn? Most men want to shine, but a man filled with the Holy Ghost is not interested in shining but in burning. Remember, Tom, if you are going to burn, you are like a candle – each day that you burn, you have less and less of your life to live. A man cannot be filled with the Holy Ghost and preserve himself. That man has to be willing to die for the power of God. Tom, do you want to burn, or do you want to shine? You also have to be willing to be peculiar. If you have ever noticed a bright light on a summer night, it attracts a lot of bugs. If you want to be filled with the Holy Ghost, you will attract some fruitcakes around you, but that is the price you have to pay to be filled with the Holy Ghost."

Dr. Malone said that he had never been the same man since that meeting as a young preacher. Dr. Tozer was simply telling Dr. Malone, "It is not how high you stand but how low you kneel."

No one has ever been ***Effectively Defeated By Temptation*** who was at the same moment ***Engaged Diligently In Supplication***. I have never been tempted to be critical of anybody that I had spent a half hour praying for earlier that day. Some of you think you just battle with being critical, that it is just your personality. Why don't you start praying instead of talking? It is hard to sit down with someone to have a meeting and start criticizing a person that both of you have spent an hour praying for God to bless and use.

I have never been tempted to quit after spending an hour on my face begging God to give me strength and to make me effective in my ministry. Former bus captain, did you really say, a week before you quit your bus route, "Oh, God, bless my bus kids. God, change their lives. God, make them champions for You. God, please let someone else pay the price so that can be true." No, you never did that, did you? We quit after months of prayerlessness. You may just be burnt out – burnt out of doing it all on your own. You ran out of gas because you were not supposed to be serving God in the flesh. You were supposed to be serving God in the energy of the Holy Spirit.

Let me get blunt. I have never had a man tell me that he got in his car and drove to a drug store to buy a dirty magazine while praying all the way there for victory and for God to make him a better husband to his precious wife and for God to make him a better dad! I am going to make a statement that you might have a hard time with: You never sinned once while you were sincerely praying.

If you do not believe in standards and convictions, you have probably never prayed about them. Have you ever prayed, "Lord, open my eyes and show me the truth. I want to be as close to You as I can. I want no sin. I want no junk in my life. God, if there is anything in my life between me and You, show it to me"? The problem is found in II Corinthians 10:4, *"For the weapons of our warfare are not carnal, but mighty through God to the pulling down of strong holds."* Our battle is not physical but spiritual.

In listing our spiritual weaponry and armor, the apostle said in Ephesians 6:17-18, *"And take the helmet of salvation, and the sword of the Spirit, which is the word of God:* **Praying always** *with* **all prayer** *and supplication in the Spirit, and watching thereunto with all perseverance and supplication for all saints."*

The words *"praying always with all prayer"* mean that at all times I need to be involved in all kinds of prayer. There are about eight types of prayer.

> **Individual Prayer.** Praying for myself.

> **Intercessory Prayer.** Praying for others.

> **Persistent Prayer.** I do not always get down and pray for my food and say, "Oh, God, I need this hamburger!" But I do persistently sit in front of a meal thank God that He was good enough to give it to me.

➤ **Passionate Prayer.** There are some times that I have to fall out and say, "Oh, God, this is your boy here, and I am making groanings right now. I don't even know what I'm saying, but I've got to have **something!**"

➤ **Fervent Prayer.**

➤ **Fasting And Prayer.** Fasting is the prayer that breaks bondage, tears down strong holds, and sets captives free. If you do not have the character to push away food for twenty-four hours, you sure do not have the character to resist temptation. God showed me that not only is prayer the source of our strength, but it is also a good practice that develops discipline. The more disciplined one is in prayer, the more disciplined he is in everything.

➤ **Secret Prayer.** The Bible says that we are supposed to find a closet, a place to go secretly and pray.

➤ **Public Prayer.**

Dear reader, where is most of your temptation? Is it in the public realm, or is it in the secret realm? None of you men that battle with pornography have a dirty magazine on your dashboard when you pull into the church parking lot. However, if you are asked to pray, you march up and put out as good a prayer as anyone. It is those secret places, those hidden chambers of our imagery (Ezekiel 8:12), where the real warfare takes place.

Here is a great principle. What you are doing in secret is a reflection of what you are not doing in secret. If you are a pervert in secret, then you do not pray in secret. But if you pray in secret, then you are not a pervert in secret. Whatever you do in secret is the opposite of what you do not do in secret.

Tragically, a preacher told me that a good, godly lady in a church, who had a good family and husband, had a total stranger send her a $3,000 computer with a camera on top of it. She started getting estranged from her husband. One day one of her daughters came in to check something on the computer. Mom had forgotten to take care of things on the computer, and when her daughter sat down, up popped a bunch of naked pictures of her mother. She was sending them to the pervert she met online who had bought her the computer. She is going to walk out on a good, Godly husband that loves her and has helped her raise her children for some pervert that she met on the Internet? She does not even know who he is. For all she knows, he could be a serial killer!

> *What You Are Doing in secret is a reflection of What You Are Not Doing in secret.*

Some of you need to pray the death of God on your computer. If you have a suspicion of something strange going on with your spouse, you suspicion is probably accurate. If your spouse tells you that you do not have to worry about anything, then he or she is probably guilty of something.

WE MUST UNLEASH THE ENERGY

Because thou hast kept the word of my patience, ***I also will keep thee from the hour of temptation,*** *which shall come upon all the world, to try them that dwell upon the earth.* **Revelation 3:10**

Confess your faults one to another, and pray one for another, that ye may be healed. ***The effectual fervent prayer of a righteous man availeth much.***" **James 5:16**

These verses imply that there is an energy that is unleashed by an effectual, fervent prayer. It is the energy to resist temptation. It is the energy to remain true to my vows, true to my commitments, true to my testimony, true to my Lord, and true to my salvation. Jesus said in our text, *"Watch and pray, that ye enter not into temptation: the spirit indeed is willing, but the flesh is weak."* The flesh is weak in two specific areas:

1. The Flesh Is Weak In Fighting Wickedness, Or Sins Of The Flesh.

➢ **Materialism.** Some dear ladies have not had one lustful thought in your life except for clothing. There is no man that occupies your lust, but your JCPenney's card is charged to the hilt. Your Marshall's card is charged to the hilt. God forbid that your husband would ever see the bill. I know good servants of God who have been crippled because their wives were spending out of control. Is that your temptation, lady?

➤ **Pride.** You do know that *"only by pride cometh contention"* (Proverbs 13:10). The fact that you cannot get along with everybody does not mean that they are all wrong. It may mean that you are all wrong.

➤ **Self-Centeredness.** Many of God's people are tempted in this area. They say, "I can't do that. I have to take care of me. I can't give there. I have to take care of me."

➤ **Laziness.** I know a lot of Christians that are tempted to be lazy. College-aged men and women better get laziness under control, or some preacher will be telling stories about them someday that they will not want to hear. He will be describing a loser who blew a great chance.

➤ **Anger.** For some, the devil does not have to do much to push your buttons, and you turn into a raging inferno. Anger is a generational curse that affects many men – angry men, like their angry fathers, out of control. My dear friend, if there are holes in your drywall, it does not mean that you are in charge; it means that you are out of control. If the only way can get your wife to submit to you is to intimidate her, shame on you! Some of you have even been so careless as to raise your hand against your wife.

➤ **Bitterness.** Many people are tempted to be bitter. They walk around with a chip on their shoulder. The devil has them in a position of such insecurity and struggling that as soon as they get hurt just a little bit, they become bitter at everybody.

➢ **Sexual Lust.**

➢ **Envy.**

➢ **Gluttony.** Gluttony is simply eating more than you need.

➢ **Dishonesty.** With some people, you do not know if they are telling the truth. If their mouth is moving, there is a good chance that they are lying.

Our flesh is weak in fighting wickedness, these sins of the flesh. You will never strengthen your will to the point that you can overcome these temptations by willpower alone. The stronger you try to be in fighting temptation in your willpower, the stronger you make your flesh! This is true because the Bible says in Jeremiah 17:9, *"The heart is deceitful above all things, and desperately wicked: who can know it?"* You will never get your old nature to be spiritual. It may fake it for a while, but there is something in your old nature that is innately wicked. The Bible says in Ecclesiastes 9:3, *"This is an evil among all things that are done under the sun, that there is one event unto all: yea, also the heart of the sons of men is full of evil, and madness is in their heart while they live, and after that they go to the dead."* You will never conquer temptation in the energy of your flesh.

Jesus confirmed this in Mark 7:21-23 when he said,

For from within, out of the heart of men, proceed evil thoughts, adulteries, fornications, murders, Thefts, covetousness, wickedness, deceit, lasciviousness, an evil eye, blasphemy, pride, foolishness: All these evil things come from within, and defile the man.

Do you think you are going to stop all those evil things by making your old nature stronger? No, Jesus said three times, *"Watch and pray."* You had better get a hold of this prayer thing, or you will never whip the filth coming out of your life. When we try to resist temptation by the willpower that we have, we strengthen the flesh, which weakens our fight.

2. The Flesh Is Weak In Fighting Weariness, Or Sins Of Fatigue.

We all understand temptation in the realm of fighting wickedness, but what about in the realm of fighting sins of weariness or fatigue? When I yield to sins of the flesh, I *Strike Out*; but when I yield to sins of fatigue, I *Opt Out*! What difference does it make? In both cases, I lose. There are many people who are not battling with temptations like pornography. A long time ago, you were tempted to quit, and you did it. You handed in your Sunday school book. You handed in your bus roster. You handed in your being a deacon. You handed in your usher job. You handed in your nursery job. You say, "But I'm still saved." I am not talking about being saved; I am talking about whipping the devil. I need energy to say, "no" when I am weak and energy to say, "yes" when I am weary.

When I get up on Monday mornings at 4:30 to travel, my flesh does not want to get up, but God has called me to do some things. I want to please the One who saved me. I do not want to please myself. I am not real good, but He is awesome! When that alarm goes off, I do not say, "Whoopee! Ha! Ha! Honey, it's 4:30!" Usually my wife has to say, "Honey, get up or you will miss your ride." I drag out of bed and wander into the bathroom, look in the mirror and say, "Who is that in the mirror?! There's a stranger in the house!" I climb in the shower, wash my old flesh off, try to put a little deodorant on, and somebody pulls in the driveway to pick me up. As I get in the car, I say, "Boy, it's good to see you!" Or should I say I wished I did?

I cannot tell you how many times, while I was running around trying to help other churches, that I have said, "Lord, I am all done doing this. Here's the baton." He says, "There is nobody here to hand it to." Usually it is that night that heaven comes down, and glory fills the church. A bunch of people will say, "Preacher, we don't know what we would have done without your coming. You have no idea. Tell your folks that we love them. Thank them for the sacrifice." I wander back to my lonely motel room and say, "Lord, thank you for the strength to do it another day."

> *When you yield to sins of the flesh, you* **Strike Out;** *when you yield to sins of fatigue, you* **Opt Out!**

A preacher called me on Christmas Eve several years ago

and said, "Preacher, I want you to do our watch night service. I talked to your secretary, and you are not having a New Year's Eve service. I want you to come and preach my watch night service."

I said, "Preacher, listen to me, listen to me real close. No. I have preached enough this year. I am worn out. My family has not seen me enough. My family is going to see me. I am not coming to your church."

He said, "Preacher, you have to come. We have to have you!"

I said, "I'll tell you what I'll do. I am going to get all my kids and my wife together. If they all agree, you have to pay for all of us to come. The only way I'll come is if my whole family agrees to it and wants to come. If they say no, I am not coming. It has nothing to do with being spiritual or not spiritual."

I asked the family, and they said, "No, we have shared you with enough people this year. We want you for the holidays."

I called the preacher back and said, "I love you, preacher, but I am not coming."

He said, "What is the first date you have at the beginning of the year?"

I said, "You are not going to leave me alone, are you?"

He said, "We have to have you. We have to have you."

I told him that I had a Thursday and Friday. I went there not knowing what to expect. I preached my heart out for two nights, got on the plane and came home on Saturday. I received a phone message from that preacher. He said, "Brother Jenkins, our church is absolutely overwhelmed. We had fifteen teenagers out soul winning Wednesday night for the first time ever. They knocked on one hundred doors. I have a deacon in my church who has been in the church for sixty-two years who came to me and said, 'Pastor, this is the greatest meeting we have had in sixty-two years.' Brother Jenkins, only heaven will tell what these two days meant to our church."

When I hear things like that, I say, "Okay, God." I am not any different than you. I have what God has put on my plate; you have what He has put on your plate. It is all different. But, are you tempted to quit? Are you tempted to pack it in? Are you tempted to go in conservation mode instead of doing all you can while you can for everybody you can to reach everybody every way you can for the Gospel?

We are not just tempted in the area of wickedness; we are tempted in the area of weariness. We all eventually run out of gas in life, but some of you have not run out quite as quickly as you would like others to think you have. Galatians 6:9 commands us, *"And let us not be weary in well doing: for in due season we shall reap, if we faint not."* II Thessalonians 3:13 says, *"But ye, brethren, be not weary in well doing."*

The Bible word for quit is *faint*. Do you know why people faint? They faint because of discouragement, disappointment, defeat, depression, or despondency? Proverbs 24:10 tells us why we faint: *"If thou faint in the day of adversity, thy strength is small."* You should study that word *adversity* in Proverbs; it literally means *"vexing"*. This word *"Vexing"* means "tempted." The wise man of Proverbs said that you quit in the day of vexing because your strength is small. In Luke 18:1 Jesus said, *"that men ought always to pray, and not to faint."*

Going on a vacation is not going to fix the problem. It might not be a bad idea, but the only thing that will give you your strength back is saying, "God, I don't have enough strength to go on. You have to help me, Lord." The Lord says, "I've been waiting to plug you in. I've been waiting for you to come by to let me recharge you." We have to unleash the energy. The energy comes from plugging into heaven in this area of prayer. I do not know how to say it any simpler. We are battling with temptation and losing because we are not praying.

We Must Utilize The Escape

> *There hath no temptation taken you but such as is common to man: but God is faithful, who will not suffer you to be tempted above that ye are able; but will with the temptation also make a way to escape, that ye may be able to bear it.* **I Corinthians 10:13**

We not only have to understand the exhortation to *"watch and pray, lest ye enter into temptation"*, we not only have to unleash the energy that the Lord knows how to deliver the godly out of temptation, but we also have to utilize our escape.

> *The Lord knoweth how to deliver the godly out of temptations, and to reserve the unjust unto the day of judgment to be punished.* **II Peter 2:9**

Just like there is a hell for those that are lost, there is an escape route for those who are saved when they face temptation. Not one of us *has* to fall to temptation. If you do not pray, you have a three-fold problem:

1. *You will not know what to say when you are tempted.*
2. *You probably will not even know that you are being tempted until it is too late.*
3. *You will not have the strength and willpower to say no.*

➢ **What settings are you in when you fall?** Avoid them. Think about the places where you struggle the most. If you struggle with being critical, who are you around? What restaurant and what coffee and what time of the week is it where you always have that temptation? Stop going there!

➢ **What props do you have that support your sin?** Eliminate them. I had an individual come to me and say, "Preacher, should I get rid of the Internet?" I said, "The fact that you are asking me answers your question. If you have to ask, you know you should." The individual cut the cord. He decided what props were supporting his sin. That will not get rid of it all, but it will sure help your praying. I am against dirty bookstores because if there were no dirty bookstores and no Internet, no matter how much you battle, you would not have a way to go after it.

> **What people are you usually with when you fall?** Avoid them.

You have to ask Jesus to help you. You have to look for the way to escape as the great hymn reads,

> Yield not to temptation, for yielding is sin,
>   Each vict'ry will help you some other to win;
> Fight manfully onward, dark passions subdue,
>   Look ever to Jesus, He will carry you through.
> Ask the Savior to help you,
>   Comfort, strengthen, and keep you,
> He is willing to aid you, He **will** carry you through.

This true story was reported in <u>The Denver Post</u>: Like many sheep ranchers in the West, Lexy Fowler had tried just about everything to stop crafty coyotes from killing her sheep. She used odor spray, electric fences, and scare-coyotes. She even slept with her lambs during the summer and placed battery-operated radios near them. She corralled them at night and herded them in at day. But every year, she lost fifty to one hundred lambs, no matter what she tried.

Then she discovered llamas. She discovered that llamas were aggressive. She also discovered that they are funny-looking and afraid of nothing. She said that when a coyote would appear around her lambs, the inquisitive llama would walk right toward it with its head up high, which the coyote translated as aggressive behavior and would head straight toward the woods. After Lexy Fowler acquired a couple of llamas, her lamb deaths went down to only three or four a year.

Some of you need to pray that God would make you a spiritual llama. Some of you already spit, and that is what llamas do anyway. They spit and bite people. Every time old slew foot comes around, every time some old dirty temptation comes around, just walk right over and say, "What are you doing around my son? What are you doing around my wife? What are you doing around my mind? Don't you understand that I am a child of God? I am not going to tolerate this!" We need to get a little more aggressive in looking for, and utilizing, our escape route.

The problem is that coyotes are opportunists, and the llamas take that opportunity away. As fearful as the devil seems, he is only an opportunist. He waits until you are alone, like Eve. He waits until you are tired and weary and maybe in a little financial trouble, like Mr. Naboth, and tries to get you to sell your heritage. He waits until a drunken party is going on to say to you, like Queen Vashti, "Go ahead and let your guard down and show your beauty to the king's friends." He comes to a weary, old, leather-lunged, giving-it-the-best-he-has John the Baptist and says, "John, do you really need to be such a hard-headed, old-fashioned, wilderness preacher? Is it really necessary for you to preach against everything? After all, this preaching against Herod is going to get you in big trouble."

If John would have been the average Bible-believing preacher today, he would have said, "You know, I am getting old. I am going to retire soon anyway. I could probably back off a little bit." But, oh no, John said, "Listen, devil, I am going to tell it to you real straight. Herod is a lousy whoremonger, and the first chance I get, I am going to tell him so." The devil said, "Well, there isn't any use talking to this old boy. The only way to shut him up is to cut his head off, because we can't cut his tongue out. He won't quit using it." And even after they cut John's head off, Herod heard about the miracles of Jesus and quit sleeping at night for fear that John was still working his business preaching against sin. I would like the devil to be disgusted with you and I to the point that he does not even know why to try anymore because we just will not stop fighting and resisting and trying to do right.

> *The devil is not afraid of our Human Performance, but he is petrified when Heaven is Petitioned!*

Far too many of God's people live in fear instead of with a will to fight. Far too many of God's people are victims instead of victors. Far too many of God's people are being overcome instead of being over-comers. James 4:7 says very plainly, *"Submit yourselves therefore to God. Resist the devil, and he will flee from you."* You say, "Well, I tried to resist the devil. I put a cross on my desk, and I put my Bible out there. Whenever I have bad thoughts I say, 'Jesus, Jesus, Jesus, blood, blood, blood, blood'." And you did it all the way to your sin, didn't you? It did not work. That is not resisting. You have been watching too many horror shows if you think that putting up a cross is going to scare the devil.

We resist the devil by saying, "Oh, God, I am so sorry and so selfish and so prone to wander. God, You have to help me! God, I want to submit to You afresh and anew today. God, You have to help me because I know that out there today there is going to be temptation bigger than me." God says, "Not now. You just called in reinforcements." The devil is not at all intimidated about your human performance, but he is petrified when heaven is petitioned and reinforcements come. Maybe this is what Paul meant when he said, *"When I am weak, then am I strong"* (II Corinthians 12:10). You see, it is not how **Tall you Stand**; it is how **Low you Kneel**. It is not how **Eloquent your Speech**; it is how **Earnest your Supplication**. It is now how **Polished your Personality**; it is how **Persistent your Prayer life**.

Could I beg you to believe these truths? The battle is not ours; it is the Lord's. We are simply pawns in a fight between good and evil, between light and darkness, between heaven and hell, between the devil and the God of our salvation.

4

The Power of Endurance

Abiding in Christ turns weakness under pressure into victorious resolve.

Wherefore let him that thinketh he standeth take heed lest he fall. There hath no temptation taken you but such as is common to man: but God is faithful, who will not suffer you to be tempted above that ye are able; but will with the temptation also make a way to escape, that ye may be able to bear it. **I Corinthians 10:12**

As you learn increasingly more about temptation, you begin feeling more and more confident about facing it and dealing with it. However, you must understand that there is something about temptation that is so sinister. Victory is not as sure as it seems. Temptation is the devil's backyard; it is where he plays most of the time. You see, he has gotten good at the game, and he does not like to lose at it. Just because you are learning and discovering some of the deeper aspects of this issue of temptation does not mean that your confidence should increase. God said,

"If you think you stand, look out! You're about to stumble." I did not say that to frighten you. If you have fallen and blundered and made some mistakes, dust yourself off, stand back up, and see what more you can learn on this subject.

As you struggle with temptation, you need to quit thinking that nobody understands what you are going through. As a matter of fact, the darker the temptation, the more people who struggle with it. More people know what you are going through than want to admit it. The devil wants you to think you are the only one that has ever faced your particular temptation. Rest assured that because we are all sinners, many share in your same struggle.

That word *bear* in verse 13 carries the same meaning as the word *endure*. If you do not want to be tempted anymore, then do not try to do anything for God. God has not promised to take away temptation. The disciples heard Jesus teach them to pray *"lead us not into temptation."* It is okay for you to pray, "Father, Abba, could we have a day without any temptations?" He may grant you that request. He may have so much for you to do this day that He will not let the devil mess with you. However, many days in your Christian life when you ask God not to let you face temptation, He is going to say, "I am going to deny that request. You need to face some temptation today." Although He loves you, He allows the devil to have access to you because He does not think the devil is going to win all the time. He gets a great deal of pleasure out of watching the devil running with his tail between his legs back toward the flames of hell. He wants you to start winning. It brings great pleasure and joy to Him when the devil finds out that His grace is sufficient.

God knows how you are going to handle the temptation. He also knows that the devil is neither omnipresent nor omniscient; and, therefore, does not know how you are going to handle it. The Bible makes this promise: When God allows those temptations to come, He is a good, just, merciful, gracious and faithful God; and He will make a way to escape every time, *"that ye may be able to bear"* or endure the temptation.

In Mark 4:17 we read, *"And have no root in themselves, and so endure but for a time: afterward, when affliction or persecution ariseth for the word's sake, immediately they are offended."* The definition of the word offended is "to be enticed, to be caused to stumble or fall away." It is literally another word for temptation. Now, understanding this meaning, consider the verse again. Child of God, how is your endurance?

In this chapter we are going to discuss **Temptation and the Power of Endurance.** You are not going to stop temptation from coming. No matter how spiritual you get or how high your standards are, you are not going to stop it. As soon as you stop making provision in one area, the devil is going to sidestep it and come at you another way.

Here is how the devil works. Maybe he deals with you, men, with an immoral thought, dishonesty, or some other sin of the flesh like that. So, you pray, labor, get counsel, and begin to lick it. Then you begin to get proud about it, and he comes after you with the temptation of pride. He never stops. He will stop when he is in hell. Until then, we just have to fight with him. God the Father is not always going to let you escape temptation, but He will give you the strength to endure temptation without yielding.

We are going to deal with the power of your new man as opposed to the power of your old man. The Scriptures say in Colossians 3:9, *"Lie not one to another, seeing that ye have put off the old man with his deeds; And have put on the new man, which is renewed in knowledge after the image of him that created him."* I have to put off the old man and put on the new man if I hope to endure temptation. You are never going to win the battle in this arena with sheer willpower. I Corinthians 10:12 is absolutely true. If you think you stand, take heed lest you fall.

So many people are frustrated and angry with themselves because they do not know why they fall. They do not know why they stumble. They look in the mirror and say, "What in the name of God is wrong with me?" If we are not careful, we will say, "By the grace of God, I am going to lick this thing." That, my friend, is exactly what the devil wants us to say, because as long as I keep trying, he is going to keep coming up with a new trick I have not considered.

Historian Shelby Foot tells of a soldier who was wounded at the Battle of Shiloh during the American Civil War and was ordered to go to the rear. The fighting was fierce, and within minutes he returned to his commanding officer. "Captain, give me a gun!" he shouted, "This fight ain't got any rear!"

Listen, child of God, this fighting we are in "ain't got any rear." There is no place to bivouac. Until Jesus comes, it is war everywhere you turn. It is bloody ground everywhere you walk. There is no rear in this fight. You have to stay in the front line with a gun in your hand and a Bible in your heart. Do you understand the armor in Ephesians chapter six? There is no armor for your backside because there is no retreat. If you try to retreat, you will face immediate defeat. You have to stand up on your feet and fight! Tomorrow is the first day of the bloodiest battle of your Christian life! There is no day you can take off. There is no hour you can get casual. There is no rear in this outfit. The fight is on!

> *Tomorrow is the first day of the bloodiest battle of your life!*

Think for a minute about David. David got up early the day he beat Goliath, but the day that Bathsheba beat him, he slept in. The lesson to be learned is that the pressure will not let up until the trumpet sounds and you are moving through the air. At that point you can say, "Farewell, farewell, sweet hour of prayer." Until that day, you are in the fight of your life, child of God.

Satan never stops trying to convince us that temporal paths, practices, or pleasures will have no eternal effects. For this reason, we need to consider three aspects involved in **The Power to Endure Temptation:**

THE VALLEY OF PRESSURE

Multitudes, multitudes in the valley of decision: for the day of the LORD is near in the valley of decision. **Joel 3:14**

In the third chapter of his prophecy, Joel identifies a period in time that the Bible calls *"the day of the LORD."* To better understand what Joel is talking about, we must realize that this time period begins after the rapture of the church, continues through the tribulation period, and ends with the one thousand year millennial reign of Christ. At the end of that reign, Satan and his demons are going to be let out of the bottomless pit to deceive the nations. Following that brief period of time, the Great White Throne Judgment is going to begin. The period of time from the rapture to the Great White Throne Judgment is what Joel is referring to as *"the day of the LORD."*

There is some debate as to what Joel was thinking when he called this time the valley of decision. But of this much we are sure: At the end of this thousand year reign, multitudes will be in the *valley of decision* because they will have to decide whether to follow the perfect, holy God who has ruled them for a millennium or to follow the temporary charlatan, the devil, who has been let loose. Joel calls this time of temptation at the end of the millennial reign of Christ the *valley of decision.*

Each and every day, multitudes face the same pressure. The first Adam faced it, and the second Adam faced it. Job called it the Valley of Decision; I call it the *Valley of Pressure.* When the first Adam was in the valley of decision he relented, he yielded, and he lost. The second Adam, in His hour of temptation, did not relent. He did not yield. Instead, He resisted and endured the temptation to yield in the wilderness, in the Garden of Gethsemane, and on the old rugged cross. Furthermore, He is sitting today on the right hand of God the Father a conqueror, because of His endurance. His battle was not an easy one. Three times the devil came after Him in the wilderness. Three times He went deeper into prayer in the garden. The Bible says He *"was in all points tempted like as we are, yet without sin"* (Hebrews 4:15). He endured the Valley of Pressure.

Most of us could whip our temptations if they happened on mountaintops. In the middle of a conference when God shows up and power is everywhere, we are not tempted to do wrong. I prepare a spiritual rendezvous with God right after Camp Meeting every year. Our annual Camp Meeting is the highlight of our calendar. The theme song of one of our teen CD's is "That's What This Altar Is For." The picture on the front cover is from Camp Meeting 2004 when nearly everyone was kneeling at the altar with tears in their eyes. Heaven had come down, and glory had filled our souls. Many had experienced great victory on this mountaintop. In spite of this time of great triumph, there were probably some men in that meeting that went out and looked at pornography the next week. We are most vulnerable right after an incredible victory.

You have to understand that it is a *valley* of pressure, not a *mountain*. He did not say multitudes on the *mountaintop* of decision; he said multitudes in the *valley*. Most of our temptation

> *Most of our temptation takes place when we are at our lowest points.*

takes place when we are at our lowest points. The devil wants to talk to us when we do not have anyone else to talk to. I never want to be critical of other people when everything is going great. He waits until I am struggling to come by and say, "Let's talk about old Bob. What are we going to do about Bob?" We cannot stay on the mountaintop everyday, so we have to learn how to endure the ***Valley of Pressure***. Every man, every day, faces the same valley of pressure.

> *Looking unto Jesus the author and finisher of our faith; who for the joy that was set before him endured the cross, despising the shame, and is set down at the right hand of the throne of God. For consider him that endured such contradiction of sinners against himself, lest ye be wearied and faint in your minds. Ye have not yet resisted unto blood, striving against sin.* **Hebrews 12:2-4**

This last verse means that you have not yet resisted the devil like Jesus resisted the devil. Again I say that the devil took Jesus to the end of the fight. He took Him to the last count. He took Him to the ropes. Even though our Lord never sinned, yielded or relented, you would be a fool to think that it was an easy fight He faced. He fought greater temptation than you or I will ever dream of facing because we are not nearly the threat to the kingdom of the devil that He was, yet He still endured the temptation without sin. He endured great contradiction of sinners against Himself. How did He do it? He resisted.

James 4:7 says, *"Submit yourselves therefore to God. Resist the devil, and he will flee from you."* We always read the "resist the devil" part and forget the first part of the verse that says, "Submit yourselves therefore to God." For the first three years of Jesus' ministry, He submitted Himself to God the Father. At one point, He says that He did everything that God told Him to do. He did nothing of His own will. Everything He did was the

Father's will.

Then in the last hour of His life, He faced the greatest temptation – the devil. He resisted Him because He spent three years drawing nigh to God. Three times in the Garden of Gethsemane He had the power to resist. I wonder if it takes one year of drawing nigh to God for every one victory in our lives. We are twenty-first century Christians. We do not want to work or labor at anything. We want it now, and if we do not get it now, we do not think it is real.

Matthew 4:10-11 says, *"Then saith Jesus unto him, Get thee hence, Satan: for it is written, Thou shalt worship the Lord thy God, and him only shalt thou serve. Then the devil leaveth him . . ."* We see that Jesus used the spiritual weapons of the Powerful Scriptures and Prayer and Supplication to resist Satan.

1. Defeating Temptation Takes Spiritual Perception.

Do you have enough sense to know when the devil is messing with you? Or, do you just wake up on the ground wondering how you got knocked out again? Luke 20:23 says of our Saviour, *"But he perceived their craftiness, and said unto them, Why tempt ye me?"*

Young people, I wonder what it would do to your youth group if, when someone was messing with you, you would look at them and say, "Why are you tempting me to disobey my parents? Why are you tempting me to listen to something that you and I both know is not God's will?" But, the average American Christian is 3,000 miles wide and one inch deep. On the surface you look good, but there is nothing to you.

When someone tries to criticize the youth director in your presence, young person, do you have enough discernment to say, "Whoa, whoa, whoa! Time out here! Are you trying to tempt me to be critical of my youth pastor?" Acting that way would not be unkind. It is the right thing to do when you are getting set up to do wrong.

How do you sit down with a couple to have fellowship over a cup of coffee and within half an hour start talking about the people you love the most as if they were your enemies? You start talking that way because you do not have any spiritual perception. About a third of the way in, you should say, "Time out!"

> *The average American Christian is 3,000 miles wide and one inch deep.*

I Corinthians 10:13 says that God is faithful and **will** make a way to escape. Do you look for those ways of escape, or do you just walk along like a blind man day after day? The question is posed in Proverbs, "How do you set a snare in the sight of a bird?" A bird gets caught in a snare because he is not very smart. He has an instinct bigger than his brain called hunger.

When I was a boy growing up in Lansing, Michigan, my buddy and I discovered a way to catch birds. We would put bread or seed under a box and prop it up with a stick under one side attached to a rope. When the birds would come up to the box, we would pull the rope, the box would fall, and the bird would be caught. Does it not bother you that you have been saved for ten, fifteen, or twenty years, and you are still getting caught under the box? You say, "I think I am not saved." You might not be saved, but maybe you are saved, and you just do not have any sense. You are too trusting. You are not supposed to be trusting of everything. There are some things that are okay to hate. Proverbs 8:13 says, *"The evil way. . . . I hate."* I preached a sermon years ago entitled "A Christian's Hate Life." I had somebody get mad at me and walk out during the service. I used the Bible to prove the things a Christian should hate. Following is a list of some evil things that I hate:

- ➢ Pornography
- ➢ Drugs
- ➢ Alcohol
- ➢ Marijuana
- ➢ Sexual abuse

In addition, I hate every kind of vice that would hurt and maim that which is holy and pure. Furthermore, it is hard to just hate the sin and not the peddler of that sin. It is absolutely necessary to get some perception in this matter. Not everybody that whispers in your ear and pats you on the back loves you. They might be acting friendly while at the same time be taking your wallet out of your back pocket. When we were on a trip to Hawaii, my wife had a lady kindly walk up and ask her for directions. While my wife gave the lady directions, she stole my wife's cell phone. Not everybody that smiles at you is going to take you to heaven. Defeating temptation takes **Spiritual Perception.**

2. Defeating Temptation Takes Supplication In Prayer.

Watch and pray, that ye enter not into temptation: the spirit indeed is willing, but the flesh is weak.
 Matthew 26:41

And he spake a parable unto them to this end, that men ought always to pray, and not to faint. **Luke 18:1**

If thou faint in the day of adversity, thy strength is small.
Proverbs 24:10

We are to pray always so we do not faint. If you do faint, it means your strength is small. The fact that we keep losing the battle of temptation means that our prayer life is lacking. We can talk about praying, but the fact is that we are not praying. When it comes to temptation, there is no evidence of prayerlessness any more powerful than failure.

No man has ever driven to a drug store to buy a dirty magazine and prayed on the way for God to make him a better husband, to bless his marriage, and to make his children holy and pure and separated. When a man goes to a drug store to buy a dirty magazine, he turns prayer off and hopes that God is not within one hundred miles of him because he knows there is going to have to be some heavy repenting to get over what he is about to do.

Failure over and over again is called presumptuous sin. God will give some mercy when people stumble and fall, but presumptuous sin makes God angry. Presumptuous sin says ,"I'm saved, and I can't lose it, so I'm going to sin anyway." You may think you got away with it before, but you keep going back to it. That sin put hooks in you, and you cannot get free. You are a defeated human disaster, dreading every moment that the public will find out who you really are.

Over the years I have counseled men who battled pornography, and they never wanted their daughters to find out about it. They promised me almost anything to not tell their daughters because the sin is so shameful. Does it not bother you that the devil keeps making a fool out of you? The devil wants you to just try harder. Instead, why don't you start praying? When you are praying, you are begging, and **God** is doing the fixing and the answering. But when you are trying harder, God does not even have to be around and often is not.

3. Defeating Temptation Takes Strength Of Purpose.

But they that will be rich fall into temptation and a snare, and into many foolish and hurtful lusts, which drown men in destruction and perdition. **I Timothy 6:9**

A. For The Businessman:

Is it wrong to want to be rich? No, it is just dangerous. That does not mean that you should not want more money. You just need to realize the danger that comes with prosperity and progress. I do not have a desire to have more money, but I have a desire to have more people. It is the same kind of issue. You may be a businessman that wants to have God prosper and grow your business. It is not wrong to want God to prosper you, but it is dangerous to want it. It is dangerous because the devil does not want any of God's children to be successful at anything. *"But they that will be rich fall into temptation . . ."* It is dangerous to want to have more and do better.

I have heard it preached all my life that it is wrong to have a lot of money. It is not wrong to have money; however, it is wrong to think you can move forward without having a bigger devil after you. So many people who have a lot of money fall out spiritually because they do not realize the danger of having money. One of the results of having a lot of money is that you start looking over your shoulder all the time. Many people that have money are lonely and easily offended; they do not feel like they have any friends. These feelings are just a resulting danger that comes with financial prosperity.

B. *For The Young Person:*

When I counsel with young people and ask them what they want to do with their lives, I would like to hear them say, "Well, I believe **God** wants me to do this." What scares me is when they say, "Well, **I** want to do this." God has not called every young man to be a preacher. However, every young person needs to make sure that whatever he does with his life is what God wants him to do. If God wants you to be a plumber, be the best plumber you can be. If God wants you to be a truck driver, be the best truck driver you can be. Just make sure that whatever you are is what *God* wants you to be and not what *you* want to be. If you are right with God, He will give you the desires of your heart. This concept does not mean that you will get what you want; it means that He will give you the right wants.

C. For The Church Member:

At the time of this writing, our church is experiencing growth in every ministry. If we want the progress, we have to be willing to understand this concept: The minute we step onto Satan's un-surrendered turf, unwilling to yield, he puts up a fight. There are some people that are not willing to pay the price to be in a church like ours. They would rather be in a church of twenty people where they get bottle-fed and burped. They want to be the center of their preacher's every thought. They are not willing to be in a church where they have to share their preacher with eight or nine hundred other people. Who does not love their preacher and want to be with their preacher? Would you rather be in a great ministry or say, "No, I don't want that. I want to have us four and no more and have the preacher belong to just me." Is this attitude wrong? No, but there is a danger in it. We can start to think that the preacher does not love us because he does not go out to coffee with us every week. The devil is going to throw temptations at a guy in a going and growing church that a guy in a church of twenty would never even think about. That is why some people say, "This church is too big for me." They are really saying that they do not want to face that pressure. They want to be in a simple Christian experience rather than in a church that is charging the gates of hell.

In the spring program, when a bus captain is trying to go and grow, all hell breaks lose. He loses his job and his wife gets sick. He is trying to mess with the devil's kingdom, and the devil is not going to give up without a fight. What do we do? How do we endure temptation? Where do we get the power? It not only takes ***Spiritual Perception*** and ***Supplication in Prayer*** but it also takes ***Strength of Purpose.*** You have to realize, "I have set myself to do something, and I am not going to let the devil stop me."

One of the reasons that I do not want to fall is that I do not want the folks who have bailed out on God to have me as an excuse. Folks that have compromised and do not believe in the old time religion would love to see the faithful fall flat on their faces? Then they could say, "See, they are not any different than the rest of us." Though it may not sound spiritual, I have ***Strength of Purpose*** in my soul that motivates me to remain faithful. I want to do right not only because I love God, but also because I do not want to give one enemy of the Gospel an excuse to bail on Him.

In Genesis 39 we have a great illustration of ***Strength of Purpose.*** I have heard preachers criticize Joseph. I wish people would not criticize others when they have not analyzed the situation enough to know what is going on. I have heard people all my life criticize Peter, but Peter is the world record holder in walking on water. He led more people to God in the first sermon he preached than any Baptist preacher I have ever heard. Even the Catholics think Peter is a pope! Isn't it funny how some guy running twenty in Sunday school will preach a sermon and criticize the Apostle Peter? Wait a minute! Time out! Consider something before you criticize the second greatest apostle in the New Testament age! Aren't you glad the Bible does not have all of *your* mistakes written down in it? It would not be a chapter or two – it would be a whole book!

Look what Joseph went through. It was not his fault that God had a great plan for his life. When Joseph let out that little vision that something great was going to be done in his life, envy crept into his brothers' hearts. They said, *"Behold, this dreamer cometh"* (Genesis 37:19). When God puts a dream in your heart, the brethren do not like you. Joseph's brothers threw him into a pit. They feigned that he was dead and sold him to some merchantmen headed to Egypt. Potiphar bought him. Potiphar had a seductive, wicked wife who tried to tempt Joseph day after day. I have heard whole sermons preached against Joseph because he left his coat in her hand. Thank God that is all that he left in her hand! I preached a sermon called "Leaving Your Coat but Keeping Your Character." I know a lot of Christians who kept their coat, meaning that their exterior looked good, but they lost their character.

Potiphar's wife came to Joseph and said, "No one is here. We are alone in the house today. My master doesn't know what is going on. Be my lover." In response, Joseph said, *"How then can I do this great wickedness, and sin against God"* (Genesis 39:9)? I love what he did next. The Bible says that day after day she was waiting to get him. Finally, the day came when she thought she had him. She got him in a situation where it seemed he was almost ready to yield, and then the Bible says that he ran out of the house. You say, "I just don't know how to deal with my temptation." Here is the best advice I can give you: RUN! RUN! RUN! Run for your life! The Bible says to *"Flee fornication"*

(I Corinthians 6:18). It also says, *"Flee also youthful lusts...."* (II Timothy 2:22). The best response you can have to fornication, to sin, or to any temptation is to run as fast as you can. Some of you are reading this book and trying to figure out how to outwit the devil. Just run! Just run!

At the time of this writing, my dad is celebrating his fifty-fourth year in the ministry. My dad never built a huge ministry, but we are all mixed up in the way we value greatness. I have a suspicion that when we get to heaven, God will be more impressed with what my dad did in fifty-four years in some tough little places just staying by the stuff, than some of us who have seen a little bit of success but do not have enough strength to say no to temptation day by day. I would rather have our college preacher boys graduate, go to some little town halfway across the country and up a holler somewhere, and be holy, Godly men than to have a thousand in their church and fall into sin.

My mom and dad just had their forty-ninth wedding anniversary. Next January they will have been married fifty years. My dad and I recently had a very holy conversation. We were talking about a particular preacher that we both loved and respected that let the devil trip him up and ruin his testimony. We were not being critical of him; we were analyzing what happened to him because we did not want it to happen to us. My dad said something to me that I will never forget. He said, "Son, between you and me and God, I have never in over forty-some years of being married had a woman proposition me once. But the more I think about it, I don't know that I was ever looking." There probably were some women that would have taken him out of the race, but he was not looking.

When I travel, I watch the way that men who are away from their families act, and it scares me. They will flirt with the stewardess on an airplane. They will talk inappropriately with female co-workers. I will occasionally see a man in an airport having lunch with a woman co-worker. I refuse to go to lunch alone with any woman in my church. I do not care if we are talking about the presidential nomination because we are running it. Without my wife sitting right next to me, I will not do it. I am not going to ride alone in a car with any woman. I do not care if it is an emergency, I will not do it. I have even had to be careful in my traveling to say that I cannot stay in people's homes. I do not believe staying in homes is wrong, but when I am at a church, I just cannot be put in a position where I might be left at a young couple's home alone with the lady of the house. I have too much at stake. I cannot have someone say, "Well, he was at work, and his wife was home . . . Where was Brother Jenkins?" No, the conversation is not going there. If a preacher tells me that he cannot afford to put me in a motel, I will pay for it myself. My testimony is worth too much to me.

The purpose for my having standards and convictions is not that I am stronger spiritually, but rather that I am not strong, and I am not spiritual. Mark Twain once said, "There are several good protections against temptation. The surest one is cowardice." John Newton once said, "When you flee temptation, be sure you do not leave a forwarding address." Ponder that. Berry McGee said, "The thing that makes men and rivers crooked is following the line of least resistance."

The Volley Of Prinicipalities

For we wrestle not against flesh and blood, but against principalities, against powers, against the rulers of the darkness of this world, against spiritual wickedness in high places. **Ephesians 6:12**

Our fight is not with men; our fight is with the devil himself. We live every day in the valley of decision, or the valley of pressure, with multitudes of other men and women. There is volley after volley of principalities and powers being thrown our way, including every conceivable device and demonic trick. Every day you live, the devil is throwing another volley at you. In Ephesians six the most important part of armor mentioned is in verse 16. The Scripture says, *"Above all, taking the shield of faith, wherewith ye shall be able to quench all the fiery darts of the wicked."* What are those fiery darts? The fiery darts are the volleys that the principalities and powers keep hurling at you day after day. As long as we live in this world, we are going to be harassed by these principalities and powers.

We are never going to outgrow these temptations, and we are never going to get separated enough or spiritual enough to totally avoid them. This means that we can never, ever take down our guard. Brother Hyles used to preach a sermon entitled "The Root Word of Casualty is Casual." The way we become a casualty is by getting too casual.

You will probably think this is crazy. Dr. Lee Roberson, the great pastor of Highland Park Baptist Church in Chattanooga, Tennessee for forty-one years and founder of Tennessee Temple University, has this conviction: He always wears double-breasted blue suits because that is what he thinks a man of God should look like. He was with a good pastor friend of mine a couple of years ago preaching. There was a man in that church that wanted to do something nice for him. He did not know what else to do, so he said, "I think I'll wash Dr. Roberson's car when he comes."

On Sunday morning, when Dr. Roberson got to the church, my pastor friend said, "Dr. Roberson, give me the keys to your car."

He said, "Why do you need the keys to my car, brother?"

"Just give me the keys to your car, Dr. Roberson," said the preacher.

Dr. Roberson said, "Why do you need the keys to my car?"

He said, "Brother Roberson, a man in my church wants to do something for you. Give me the keys to your car."

Dr. Roberson said, "Why do you need the keys to my car?"

He said, "Dr. Roberson, one of my men wants to wash your car today."

Dr. Roberson said, "Oh, no. No, no, no. I don't believe in working on the Lord's day. I have never washed my car on Sunday in seventy-some years, and I am not starting today."

Rebuked by the man of God, my pastor friend walked underneath the door behind Dr. Roberson. Dr. Roberson had just had his mind made up that there were things that were right to do and things that were wrong to do, none of which were negotiable. Is it a sin to wash your car on Sunday? I do not think so, but I sure like a man who is not going to change his mind about what he believes.

I do not know any conviction Dr. Roberson had that I have ever admired more than the one I am about to explain. Dr. Roberson had a conviction that if he ever saw his wife in public anywhere in Chattanooga, he would not walk up to her and speak to her. If she were on a street corner needing a ride, he would not pick her up. He would go back to the church and have someone else go get her. You see, Chattanooga is a town of over 100,000 people. A lot of people in Chattanooga knew Dr. Lee Roberson, but not many people in Chattanooga knew Mrs. Lee Roberson. He never wanted the news to get around town that Lee Roberson was seen at such-and-such a corner picking up a strange woman. You might think this safeguard is too narrow-minded, but he is ninety-five and still preaching. There are a number of preachers that are slick and smooth. They are not as rigid and "legalistic" as Dr. Roberson, but they are also no longer even living for God. I am going to stick with those old timers who just drew a straight line and walked it.

Some of you need to get some things settled in your Christian life, or you are never going to whip temptation. I had a man come up to me a few weeks ago and say, "Preacher, do you think I should get rid of Internet at my house?" There has been some dispute between him and his wife about his integrity with the Internet. I said, "Why are you asking me this question?" I implied in counseling that he should get rid of it, but I do not make people do anything. I am a seed sower, not a fruit inspector. My job is done when I tell you what God wanted me to tell you. What you do is between you and God. I am going to love you whether you follow my advice or not. That session took place after my first sermon on temptation. After the second sermon, that man walked the aisle with tears in his eyes and said, "Preacher, I did it." He was saying, "I am going to quit playing games. I am going to quit acting like I can control it."

You cannot control temptation. If you can control the Internet in a private place, sir, I think you are fruitier than a three-dollar bill. Quit playing games. If you need the Internet, then make sure your computer is in a place where you can be above reproach. Make sure your computer is in a place where anybody can look at it and check it out. Some of you know the Internet well enough that you can fake people out. If you are slick enough that you can fake people out, then you need to get rid of the Internet. If you know more than your wife does about the Internet, then you are above accountability in that area. Nobody in this fallen world can live above accountability in *any* area. We will fall flat on our faces. Getting above accountability is the ultimate tactic of the devil's attack. To live above accountability is what the devil tried to get Adam and Eve to do in the Garden of Eden. He told them, "The reason God is not letting you know what is going on is because He is wanting to keep you from the knowledge that will make you understand what He understands." They said, "Oh, we want that knowledge."

The best time to go deer hunting is in the rut because that

> *Getting above accountability is the ultimate tactic of the devil's attack.*

page • 127

is when the big bucks fall. During rut, the big bucks lose their caution because they are thinking about mating with does. During this time, they lose their edge. I killed two eight-point trophy bucks one year within ten minutes of each other. They were walking through the woods like they were in a parade because there were some does in the neighborhood. I shot the first one with a high-powered rifle. His brother was right behind him, oblivious to the sound. The shot of the gun did not even deter him. It does not surprise me. I see Christian men falling constantly. They watch other men fall, and it does not even deter them. You may think that you are different. You may think that you are strong. If you have this attitude, you will probably fall tomorrow. If you think you stand, take heed lest you fall.

The Victory Of Patience

"Because thou hast kept the word of my patience, I also will keep thee from the hour of temptation, which shall come upon all the world, to try them that dwell upon the earth." **Revelation 3:10**

Why do you need patience to become victorious over temptation? You cannot miss this thought. Isn't it interesting that James 1:2-4 says, *"My brethren, count it all joy when ye fall into divers temptations; Knowing this, that the trying of your faith worketh patience. But let patience have her perfect work, that ye may be perfect and entire, wanting nothing."*

In II Corinthians 12, Paul asked God to remove his thorn in the flesh. I have heard many debates about what his thorn in the flesh was. Instead of everybody arguing about what it was, we should just take Paul's word and believe what he said it was. I have heard people say that Paul's eyesight was bad or that he was weak physically. Some of that may have been part of it, but we should just take Paul's word. He said that it was *"the messenger of Satan to buffet me."* (II Corinthians 12:7). Paul said that his thorn in the flesh was a messenger of Satan. He said, "I am involved in hand to hand combat with the devil, the enemy of my soul. God, would you get him away from me? I can't take this anymore, God. I don't want to be tempted anymore." God said, "No, Paul, I will not take the messenger of Satan to buffet you away. What you need instead, Paul, is more grace." Paul wanted a reprieve, but instead God said that Paul needed a revival. God said, "You don't need less trouble. You need more trouble than you have ever had because trouble, Paul, is what keeps you right with Me."

Vacations are dangerous things because when people go on vacation, they let their guard down. Baptists do not go to the beach, they go to the shore. Preachers used to preach against going to the beach and bathing with a bunch of heathen people. We do not go to the beach anymore, we go to the shore. I am not saying that it is wrong to go to the beach to swim with your family, but do it about a mile up the beach from anybody else. If you cannot find a secluded beach, then it probably is not the will of God to go. Ladies, if that big, honest, spiritual man that you are married to says he can lie on the beach unbothered while half-naked women walk by, find a big stick and beat some sense into him! He wants you to think that it does not bother him.

We cannot expose ourselves to those kinds of things if we want to win the battle with temptation. Paul wanted to be greatly used of God. He prayed in Philippians 3:10, *"That I may know him, and the power of his resurrection, and the fellowship of his sufferings, being made conformable unto his death."* He prayed all of that before II Corinthians 12. It was in II Corinthians 12 that Paul prayed for God to take his thorn away, and God said, *"No, I am not going to get you in a place where you do not have pressure, Paul. This valley of pressure is a good thing for you, Paul. But I will give you an extra dose of Me."* Paul was asking God to remove the temptation; but instead, God gave him more of His touch on his life. Some of you are being tempted more than you have ever been tempted in your life, and it is because God's hand is on you and the devil knows it. The tragedy is that you do not know it. As long as the devil has you thinking that he is winning, he is having a party.

Hebrews 12:1 says, *"Wherefore seeing we also are compassed about with so great a cloud of witnesses, let us lay aside every weight, and the sin which doth so easily beset us, and let us run with patience the race that is set before us."* That word beset means "to trouble, to harass, to skillfully surround, or to hem in." Every one of us has some sin, some trouble, or some harassment in our life that seems like it has us.

Psalm 139:5 states, *"Thou hast beset me behind and before, and laid thine hand upon me."* God says that you are to lay aside that sin that so easily besets you. You have to conquer, overcome, and rid yourself of that besetting sin. David said, "The One that put that besetting sin in my life is God. God is the One that made me to have that weakness. God is the One that allowed that experience to come across my life." David said, "I am beset, and God is the One that allowed it to happen." This verse is the Old Testament illustration of a New Testament truth. Paul wanted God to remove his thorn in the flesh, and God said, "No!" The last part of Psalm 139:5 says, *"and laid thine hand upon me."* You say, "I want God to use me. I want to be a greater Christian. I want to be a greater servant of God. I want to be a greater preacher. I want to be a greater Sunday school teacher. I want to be a greater bus captain. I want to be a greater worker. I want to be a greater deacon. I want to be a greater prayer warrior. I want to be a greater soul winner. I want to be a greater dad. I want to be a greater mom. I want to be a greater Christian." Then you have to make up your mind that *if you want the touch, you will have to deal with the temptation.*

> *If you* **want the touch,** *you will have to* **deal with the temptation.**

We want the temptation to go away and the touch to come. David said that the besetting was connected to the touching. God is not the One that tempts you to sin, but God is the One that allows the temptation to happen. He has allowed you to be beset because He wants you to need Him. You can be moral and on your way to Hell because you can be moral by simply having strong character. Understand that the devil might actually help a lost man who has character to stay moral just to make him think that he does not need God because he is so good. However, if you start winning the devil's children to God and getting them to win their friends to God, and you start impacting his kingdom, he is going to say, "Where is that man's besetting sin? Let's ruin him!"

Paul said, "Oh, God, he's after me. Please get him away." And God said, "No, Paul, you do not need less of the devil; you just need more of Me." We do not want to admit it, but we are like the Catholic monks. We want God to put us in monasteries – an unrealistic place – to get victory. God put you in this world to be a witness. You have to stay in the world, but the world does not have to stay in you. Your boat can be in the water, but when the water gets in the boat, you begin to have problems. Annie Hawks wrote a poem that her pastor, Robert Lowry, put to music. It was published in the National Baptist Sunday School Convention Songbook in 1872. Here were the words she penned:

I Need Thee Every Hour

I need Thee ev'ry hour,
Most gracious Lord;
No tender voice like Thine
Can peace afford.

I need Thee, O I need Thee;
Ev'ry hour I need Thee!
O bless me now, my Saviour,
I come to Thee!

I need Thee ev'ry hour,
Stay Thou nearby;
Temptations lose their pow'r
When Thou art nigh.

I need Thee ev'ry hour,
In joy or pain;
Come quickly and abide,
Or life is vain.

I need Thee ev'ry hour,
Teach me Thy will
And thy rich promises
In me fulfill.

I need Thee ev'ry hour,
Most Holy One;
O make me Thine indeed,
Thou blessed Son!

I need Thee, O I need Thee;
Ev'ry hour I need Thee!
O bless me now, my Saviour,
I come to Thee!

When you are walking hand in hand with the Saviour, you get the power to endure temptation. The power is not in you; the power is in the message you preach. Paul said in Romans 1:16, "For I am not ashamed of the gospel of Christ: for it is the power of God." Everybody wants the power of God on his life. God says, "Why would I put my power on your life? The power of God has a message attached to it." If you are not going to tell the message, why do you need the power? That is how God's economy works. You say, "God, I want you to help me be a victorious Christian." He says, "Okay, where do I get to stay in the house?" Then you say, "Now I want you to help me defeat the devil." He says, "Okay, we are going to get up at 4:00 A.M.

tomorrow to pray."

We want the *Victory with no Labor*. We want the *Power with no Presence*. We do not want the devil around, but we really do not want God around either. Friend, you do not get rid of the devil and live in your own strength. The only way you can abide is to let God run the show. If God is not running the show, then the devil is. The power to endure is not in you or in me. I have been trying for over twenty-five years to whip some things that I am still struggling with because I do not have the power to whip them alone. The conclusion to Paul's dilemma with his thorn was this: When I am weak, then He is strong (II Corinthians 12:10).

> *We do not need less of the devil's temptation. We just need more of God!*

5

THE PITIFUL EXAMPLE

Samson's life is a tragic example of failure in temptation.

By this point in the book, you should have figured out that there are no little secrets in defeating temptation. Nothing short of a daily dependence on God, and walking daily with Him, is going to make you a victorious Christian. *"Trust and obey, for there's no other way to be happy in Jesus"* is not just good for three or four generations ago; it is good for today's generation as well.

The subject dealt with in this chapter may be just what is needed to grab your soul and conscience so that all that has been discussed to this point can become a force in your life. Are you sick and tired of getting whipped by the devil? Are you sick and tired of looking at another pile of rubble and wondering how you yielded to temptation yet again? You cannot believe you went and gossiped again. You cannot believe you fell again. You cannot believe you said that again. You wonder why you keep falling in the same places.

One of these days, I want the devil to say, "Where's Jon? We're used to his coming by here every once in a while." Well, he is not coming anymore! He figured out what you are doing, and he is not going to come around and let you harass him anymore. What a testimony that would be.

This chapter is going to deal with the tragedy of a man who was toying with temptation and who, in the end, tumbled and fell.

In Greek mythology, Achilles was the son of Peleus, king of the Myrmidons, and Thetis, a sea goddess. Achilles was the greatest, bravest, and most handsome warrior in the army. One of the tales about his childhood relates how Thetis held the young Achilles by the heel and dipped him in the waters of the River Styx. By dipping his body in the mythological waters, Achilles became invulnerable – except the heel by which he was held. From this story, we get the term "Achilles Heel." Every other part of him was invulnerable; he could not be stopped, except for his heel. There was a part of him that was weak and vulnerable.

Achilles would have been better off if more than his heel had been vulnerable. The fact that we are good at so much makes the temptations we deal with so dangerous. An arrow struck Achilles in the heel and killed him because that was where his weakness was.

Child of God, are you mature and secure enough to be honest about what *your* "Achilles Heel" is? I am not worried about that person who knows his area of weakness. I am worried about that person who is still wondering when this book will apply to him.

You may not be a drunk, a whoremonger, a woman chaser, a man chaser, or a liar. You may be thinking, "I don't know what this book is talking about. I am more spiritual than that."

The following is a list of some common "Achilles Heels," or areas of weakness, that point to an extreme vulnerability in our walk with God:

> ➤ **Pharisaism.** You think you are God's appointed policeman. You thank God you are not as bad as all the Publicans you know. People with this "Achilles Heel" are usually critical, judgmental, gossipers, and fault finders. The disciples had this mind set in Luke chapter nine. Jesus rebuked them in Luke 9:55 by saying, *"Ye know not what manner of spirit ye are of?"*

> ➤ **Money.** Some people would say, "I would never miss church on Sunday night." But, as soon as they get a job making three times more money than they have ever made, they will not be in church on Sunday night.

> ➤ **Ambition.** Sometimes in our drive to succeed, we become obsessed with more money, more influence, and more of everything. Many of God's finest have been destroyed by their own ambition. Be careful what you want. You just might get more than you bargained for.

> ➤ **Power.** Diotrophes loved to have the preeminence. It is funny how we can see another's "Achilles Heel" so well without being able to see our own. I have been around some people that bounce from church to church to church,

splitting churches and hurting people. They just have to feel important.

> **Prestige.** People with this "Achilles Heel" would do almost anything to be thought well of, even to the point of selling out.

Samson, our pitiful example, had the "Achilles Heel" of sensuality. He was a great man who had a weakness that he never dealt with. As great a man as Samson was, he melted before his passions

> *We have a tendency to toy with temptation rather than to resist it.*

when it came to women. He was a *He Man with a She Weakness*. The story of Samson's downfall at the hands of Delilah is one of the most famous stories in the entire Bible. Its blend of love, betrayal, violence, and treachery gives it all the dimensions of a classic tragedy. It has been told and retold throughout the ages. However, Samson's tragedy is not unique. Countless believers have lost their strength for the exact same reason Samson lost his.

If we are honest, we must confess that we, like Samson, have a tendency to toy with temptation rather than to resist it. We all have a tendency to trifle with sin, rather than to flee from it like the Bible commands us to *"flee also youthful lusts. . ."* (II Timothy 2:22).

Let us look at some lessons that we can learn from this pitiful example, this failure, in the life of Samson in the matter of temptation:

The Inclination Samson Fostered

Then went Samson to Gaza, and saw there an harlot, and went in unto her. And it was told the Gazites, saying, Samson is come hither. And they compassed him in, and laid wait for him all night in the gate of the city, and were quiet all the night, saying, In the morning, when it is day, we shall kill him. And Samson lay till midnight, and arose at midnight, and took the doors of the gate of the city, and the two posts, and went away with them, bar and all, and put them upon his shoulders, and carried them up to the top of an hill that is before Hebron. **Judges 16:1-3**

Remember Paul's words in I Corinthians 10:13:

There hath no temptation taken you but such as is common to man: but God is faithful, who will not suffer you to be tempted above that ye are able; but will with the temptation also make a way to escape, that ye may be able to bear it.

Samson did not fail because the temptation was too strong, and he did not fail because the temptation was inescapable. He failed because he toyed and trifled with sin. The reality is that you may know that everything in this book is true, but you will still not quit playing around with sin. You think that you can handle your temptation. Ambrose, an early Christian writer, put it like this:

> Samson, when brave, strangled a lion, but he could not strangle his own love. He burst the fetters of his foes, but not the cords of his own lusts. He burned the crops of others, and lost the fruit of his own virtue when burning with the flame enkindled by a single woman.

What a tragedy that so much strength, so much power, and so much potential was squandered and defeated by such a simple foe. The first part of Samson's downfall is not as well known as it should be. We always teach about the latter part of the chapter when Delilah took Samson out, but Delilah was not the beginning of his problems. She was the end of his problems. In this first chapter in his life, when he went down to Gaza, he went in unto an harlot. That means that he was immoral. What he sowed in Gaza with a harlot, he reaped in Sorek with Delilah. Dr. Bob Jones, Sr. said, "Behind every tragedy in human character is a long process of wicked thinking."

> *"Behind every tragedy in human character is a long process of wicked thinking."*
> Dr. Bob Jones, Sr.

Tell me about your secret world, that other life you are living, the life that you shriek to even think about because you know it is wrong. You are ashamed and embarrassed that you struggle, yet you still do.

1. Samson Dulled Himself Spiritually.

There can be no doubt that at this point in his life, Samson was totally out of fellowship with God. There was no way that he was right with God when he went down to an harlot. Apparently, he had learned absolutely nothing from his previous mistakes as recorded in Judges chapters fourteen and fifteen. This woman in Judges 16:1 was not the first woman with whom he had problems. His devotional life, as far as we can tell, was non-existent because he dulled his spiritual senses!

How is *your* devotional life? *Devotional* means that you are devoted to something. I could look in a man's garage and see what he is devoted to. I could go through a house and see what a lady is devoted to by the knick-knacks she collects. Imelda Marcos was devoted to collecting shoes; years ago, they found 7,000 pairs of shoes in her closet. That sounds like a devotion to me.

How much time do you spend every day in the Word of God? In this wicked day in which we are living, men who are in places of leadership need to read a minimum of ten chapters of the Bible a day to stay right with God. How in the world can you stay spiritual on two or three chapters of Bible a day with the devils we are facing? We are living in a very ungodly age. The temptations that are being thrown at people right now are unbelievable.

Dr. Jack Schaap of the First Baptist Church in Hammond, Indiana, said that in the number one selling Sony PlayStation game today you have to rape a woman and kill her, steal a car, kill a policeman, and urinate on him in order to win. That is the number one selling game in the country today. A mayor in the

Chicago area tried to make an issue out of this game and said that something needed to be done about it. Over two thousand letters came in to the radio broadcast telling him to mind his own business. Most of those replies came from parents. We do not want anyone telling us what to do with our children. They can play with whatever they want to play with. Is there anybody awake, or has this country gone brain-dead? I am not saying that it is a sin to have Sony PlayStation, but you should consider taking a log splitter to that game. You might have a boy that is a expert at video games, but he has not read his Bible in a month. Your boy will be a Samson someday.

Let me address the teenage boys right now. For some of you, your spiritual life is a joke. You do not walk with God at all. The only reason you look fairly spiritual is because of all the preaching you get that sort of keeps you out of trouble. Young men, you had better get a grip on this thing. The character that you are going to live with for the rest of your life is being developed right now. If you do not learn to get a hold of God with as little as you have in your schedule right now, wait until you get to be a man and have a hundred things pulling at you every day. You had better learn to walk with God!

Samson dulled himself spiritually. Do you really desire to bring others to Christ? You see, when your devotion to the Lord wanes, you lose your early fervor. The following are indicators of spiritual dullness:

- Your hunger for the Word of God begins to evaporate.

- Your prayer time grows shorter.

- You like to be around worldly things.
- The people of God embarrass you.

Friend, these indicators are flashing lights on your spiritual dashboard. You need to stop and get a check-up. Do not keep driving wondering why you are losing your fire and your zeal. Remember back to the time when what it cost to serve God really did not matter. Remember when you would spend the extra time on your bus route or the extra hour on your knees. You did not care what it cost you. You have time for all of your business deals and time to go on vacation, yet your spiritual life is growing dull.

2. Samson Defiled Himself Morally.

Every sin is a sin; there is no white or black sin. However, different sins cause different degrees of damage. Proverbs 6:32 states, *"But whoso committeth adultery with a woman lacketh understanding: he that doeth it destroyeth his own soul."* The Bible says that a man who commits a sensual, sexual, or lustful sin sins against his soul. Moral sins are sins that you do not recover from as easily as you may recover from other types of sins.

Samson went down to Gaza, saw a harlot, and went in unto her. Samson crossed a line. We see only the physical, or moral, line that he crossed; we do not see the spiritual line that he crossed. Samson was a great servant of God, one who performed great miracles and powerful feats and was led and visited by God. Does it not seem incredible that he could take his pure, holy, Nazarite body and join it unto a harlot?

When a man and woman kiss one another, they form a soul bond that is not easily broken. I like to call it a soul tie. Whenever any bodily fluid is exchanged, a soul tie is made. That is why we believe in one boy and one girl for life. You do not go shopping, try them all, and take home the one you like the best. The problem with a "shop around" attitude is that you form a soul tie with every one of those people. Some day when you flip out, you will realize that there was some invisible bondage from sinning against your soul.

What in the world was Samson thinking about? He was the judge in Israel. He was God's anointed and appointed leader, and he joined himself unto a harlot. The fact is, Samson was *not* thinking. I counseled a missionary who was involved in some moral sin and asked him, "What were you thinking?" His response was, "I wasn't, Preacher. Nobody ever thinks when he is sinning."

   A. *Samson Defiled Himself By Where He Went.*

Gaza is not where God's people are supposed to be hanging out. Gaza was forty miles from Samson's hometown of Zorah. It was one of the five chief cities of the Philistines. Samson had no business hanging out in Gaza. You are going to get in trouble if you hang out in the wrong places. It does not matter if you are drinking Pepsi, you do not need to be at the tavern playing darts. It does not matter how much you love bowling, you need to pray about being involved in a bowling league. They do not sing "Jesus Loves Me" at the bowling alley; however, an awful lot of booze gets consumed there. Sometimes it seems as if we are walking around brain-dead, falling into the same traps that others have for generations.

B. Samson Defiled Himself By What He Did.

"And he went down, and talked with the woman; and she pleased Samson well" (Judges 14:7). Notice that this area of waywardness was not a one-time event in Samson's life. He went after Delilah, he went after the harlot in Judges 16:1, and he had the same problem in Judges 14:7. This woman was a Philistine woman. Samson was always looking for the wrong kind of girl because sensuality was his besetting sin. Samson's sensuality may, at times, have been dormant, but it was never dead. He never dealt with his sensuality. He never put it on the cross. He never crucified it. He never killed it. That which you do not deal with will one day deal with you.

You will not control your flesh. Jesus said in Mark 9:43, *"And if thy hand offend thee, cut it off: it is better for thee to enter into life maimed, than having two hands to go into hell, into the fire that never shall be quenched."* He also said in Mark 9:47, *"And if thine eye offend thee, pluck it out: it is better for thee to enter into the kingdom of God with one eye, than having two eyes to be cast into hell fire."* Jesus said that you would be better to cut an arm off and get to heaven than you would be to use that arm for a wicked

> **Samson's sensuality may, at times, have been dormant, but it was never dead.**

life and end up in hell one day.

Some of you men that battle pornography should pray for blindness – it would be better than hell. The Bible says in Revelation 21:8, *"But the fearful, and unbelieving, and the abominable, and murderers, and whoremongers, and sorcerers, and idolaters, and all liars, shall have their part in the lake which burneth with fire and brimstone: which is the second death."* We believe in eternal security, but I am just telling you what the Bible says. You explain that verse any way you want to explain it. I am not saying that if you have fallen into immorality you are going to hell. I am just saying that the Bible says that whoremongers will not inherit the kingdom of God. We had better quit playing around and understand that some of these sins we have never dealt with may be sins we have never repented of. If we have not repented, we cannot believe.

> **That which you do not deal with will one day deal with you.**

See what Proverbs 6:26-29 has to say about this issue:
For by means of a whorish woman a man is brought to a piece of bread: and the adulteress will hunt for the   precious life. Can a man take fire in his bosom, and his clothes not be burned? Can one go upon hot coals, and his feet not be burned? So he that goeth in to his neighbour's wife; whosoever toucheth her shall not be innocent.

Dr. Allen Jones used to say of the sensual world in which we are living, "Men do not *fall* into the sin of sensuality, they *jump* into it." Falling implies an accident. Nobody accidentally gets involved in an immoral situation. Immorality is always premeditated.

Do you recall the little children's chorus? *"Oh, be careful little eyes what you see; Oh, be careful little feet where you go; Oh, be careful little hands what you touch. For the Father up above is looking down in love. Oh, be careful. . ."* How vigilant are you in keeping away from the *places*, *people*, and *programs* that stimulate sensuality?

> *"Men do not fall into the sin of sensuality, they jump into it."*
> Dr. Allen Jones

3. *Samson Displayed Himself Physically.*

When Samson's enemies discovered that he was with this harlot, they tried to trap him. They woke him up in the middle of the night in an attempt to slay him. In response, Samson, with his enormous strength, went out of the prostitute's house, ripped out the gates of the city from their foundations, and walked away with them on his shoulders. Verse three says that he carried them on his shoulders *"to the top of an hill that is before Hebron."* It is not great to see Samson's unusual strength; it is a tragedy.

The tragedy is that he was a man with ***Power*** but no ***Purity***. He had ***Strength*** but no ***Self-Control***. His display of strength is not impressive. There is nothing more tragic than a talented person with no character. There are so many people who have talent literally oozing out of them, and they are worth almost nothing.

Mom and Dad, be careful how you handle your children's talent. We had a teenaged girl in our church with a phenomenal singing talent, but we never allowed her to sing solos when she was in high school. We did not want to ruin her. We did not want her to get a big head. Today she is happily married to a preacher, serving the Lord. Many of our children are talented; however, if we are not careful, that talent will destroy them. As parents, we sometimes get a perverted sense of self worth when our children's talent is displayed. We think that it makes us look good. Who cares? I do not care if my child shines today; I am concerned that they are still living for God ten years from now.

Some people have talent and cannot understand why they are not being used in their church. Their character needs to catch up with their talent. It does not matter how well they sing; they will need to stop smoking before they can sing in church. Likewise, a woman needs to dress modestly and take care of herself before she can sing in church.

> **Samson had power without purity and strength without self-control.**

We all have some talent somewhere. You may not have a public talent; your talent may be more private, like sewing or cooking. Cooking is a talent that someday someone will appreciate! You may be the best homemaker ever made; the fact that homemaking may not be a public talent does not mean that you do not have a talent. Your talent, whatever it may be, will probably be the cause of your downfall, should you ever fall.

There are many people that are good at shooting from the

hip. They could sing, preach, or testify without any preparation, and you would never know they had not prepared. What a curse! What a curse to have that kind of strength. Some may think that I have that kind of strength, but I do not. Probably one of the reasons I get accused of preaching too long is because I come to the pulpit with page after page of notes. I come with so many notes because I do not want to ever get good at faking it.

> *There is nothing more tragic than a talented person with no character.*

The question that has always rung in the hearts of God's people, no doubt, has been, "Why did God not deal with Samson sooner? Why didn't God chasten him? Why didn't God remove him? Why didn't God punish him? Why was there no discipline until the end?" The only explanation that I can give you is that we have a patient God. I am thankful that God is longsuffering. God has used all of us in spite of us.

THE TEMPTATION SAMSON FACED

Samson's temptation revolved around Delilah. Actually, we know very little about her except that the Bible implies that she was beautiful and attractive to Samson, and he entered into an immoral relationship with her. *"And it came to pass afterward, that he loved a woman in the valley of Sorek, whose name was Delilah"* (Judges 16:4). This story fascinates me.

The Philistines were determined – in any way, shape, or

form – to get rid of Samson once and for all. When Samson fell for Delilah, they thought they had found their opportunity. The Philistines had five major cities. Each city had a lord, or governor over it. These five Philistine lords came to Delilah and offered her about $5,000 to discover the source of Samson's strength. The Bible says that geographically Samson found Delilah in the *Valley of Sorek*, which lay between Zorah and Timnath on the border of Judah and Philistia. It was a border town.

You will get in trouble, child of God, if you spend much time hanging around border towns. Border towns, in a literal and practical sense, are very ungodly places. Border towns are normally wicked places, but that is not the point I am trying to make. The thing that I do not like about a border town is that it is not far enough in either direction. It is a fence-straddling place. Sorek was not quite in Judah and not quite in Philistia; it was just on the border.

> *I do not care if my child shines today; I am concerned that they are still living for God ten years from now.*

Some of you just need to get in and quit hanging around halfway. It is a dangerous thing for a child of God to linger at the enemy's border. If you stay there long, you will not leave. You will get caught there.

1. The Source Of Samson's Temptation.

"And Delilah said to Samson, Tell me, I pray thee, wherein thy great strength lieth, and wherewith thou mightest be bound to afflict thee" (Judges 16:6). There are three very important principles about temptation that are embodied in Delilah:

A. She Was Attractive.

Delilah was a beautiful, attractive woman. There is nothing in the Bible that indicates otherwise. When temptation comes, it comes in attractive packages. Have you discovered that? You have never had some woman with her teeth falling out, half bald and in need of a shave tempt you, sir. If she did, you might have a problem other than sensuality. I heard one old preacher say it like this, "Satan puts poison right in the middle of a sirloin steak and invites you for supper." Satan always packages his temptations attractively.

B. She Was Seductive.

The word *Delilah* means "flirtatious" or "seductive." Delilah, whose name means seductive, comes to different people in different forms:

➤ To Noah, she came in the form of **Wine.**

"And he drank of the wine, and was drunken; and he was uncovered within his tent." **Genesis 9:21**

➤ To Uzziah, she came in the form of **Power.**

And he made in Jerusalem engines, invented by cunning men, to be on the towers and upon the bulwarks, to shoot arrows and great stones withal. And his name spread far abroad; for he was marvellously helped, till he was strong.
II Chronicles 26:15

➢ To Diotrophes, she came in the form of **Positional Preeminence**.

I wrote unto the church: but Diotrephes, who loveth to have the preeminence among them, receiveth us not.
III John 9

Not everybody battles with sensuality; sensuality is not everyone's "Achilles Heel." Understand that your adversary knows the appropriate guise in which to send his Delilah to you, and if you are trifling with it rather than fleeing from it, the result will be disastrous.

We all have an "Achilles Heel." Does it not break your heart every once in a while to hear a story of someone who has fallen? I know a preacher that took over a great church in a metropolitan city – a church with a great testimony, a church some of the best-known preachers in the country called their home church. I thought this particular church would probably triple its attendance in just a short time when this man took it over. I called him a few months after he assumed the pastorate, and he said, "God have mercy, Brother Jenkins! We are having hell by the acre. As you know, this church has had a history of great missions giving. It is a church of three or four hundred, and they are giving $300,000 a year to missions. Preacher, the financial secretary, one of the most respected ladies in the church, embezzled over one million dollars from the church over a period of fifteen years."

Not everyone battles with sensuality. This lady battled with money, with buying things. She wanted the prestige of people thinking that she always treated them right and went out of her way to love them with money. The problem was that it was not *Her* money that she loved everyone with! It was all missions money. Be careful, child of God! Just because your "Achilles Heel" may not be as ugly or as dangerous as some does not mean that it is not just as wicked. You better know what your "Achilles Heel" is, and you better deal with it. Do not play games with it.

It is important to know your strengths, but it is a life and death issue to know your weaknesses! This next statement is out of the bounds for some, but somebody other than you needs to know your weaknesses. Tell somebody your weaknesses.

> **Married People Should Tell Their Spouse Their Weaknesses.** My wife knows my weaknesses because I want to be accountable. Dear lady, you better tell your husband your weaknesses. If your mate will not tell you, ask them and tell them what you *think* their weaknesses are. That will get the conversation going! Suggest the weaknesses you think you see. You may need to have marriage counseling afterwards, but

Trifling with temptation rather than fleeing from it will result in disaster.

it is better to get back together after a fight than after a tragedy like a Samson and Delilah story.

➢ **Young People Should Tell Their Parents Their Weaknesses.** They already know your weaknesses anyway. You cannot hide anything, especially from momma. My mom could read my mind; it was almost spooky. If your child asks, "Mom, everybody is going to bed in a half hour, right?" You should think, "What is he up to?" Wait about forty-five minutes and go and see what he is up to. I thank God for that kind of vigilance! When I was a teenager, I did not appreciate it, though. There were a few nights that mom and I had a heart-to-heart talk about what I was doing. Parents, do not hide your children's weaknesses. People will find out their weaknesses whether you tell them or not. Deal with your child's weaknesses when he is young. A great preacher once said, "It is better to mend boys than to fix men."

C. *She Was Cooperative.*

Samson did not cut his own hair; someone helped him to cut it. Samson did not tie ropes around himself; someone did it for him. Samson elected to spend time around the wrong company, and they did the rest. Be careful with whom you are cooperating. Temptation comes when we choose the wrong company.

Brother Hyles used to preach a great sermon from Galatians 3:1, *"O foolish Galatians, who hath bewitched you, that ye should not obey the truth, before whose eyes Jesus Christ hath been evidently set forth, crucified among you?"* His sermon was entitled, "Who In The World Happened To You?" Brother Hyles used to say, "No one ever backslides alone; they always backslide with the help of someone or something else." Samson always chose the wrong company:

- **The Philistine Woman From Timnath** (Judges 14:1)
- **The Prostitute From Gaza** (Judges 16:1)
- **Delilah**

It was those women with whom Samson chose to spend his time that helped to destroy his character.

> *Temptation comes when we choose the wrong company.*

There is nothing that shapes our character more than the people with whom we choose to spend our time. Do you honestly ever evaluate your friendships? I not only evaluate my friendships as a person but also as a pastor. There are some preachers I have not exposed my church to for a reason. They may claim to be fundamental Baptists and may claim to be good men, but I would rather misjudge a few than to let some dynamic personality come and drift my church off into some schism somewhere. I have to be careful with whom I associate as a preacher. I will associate with a person who believes that the King James Bible is the Word of God. I do not mean that they are Textus Receptus King James men, who believe that the King James Bible is the best one. If I am going to associate with them and allow them to influence my church, they better believe that the King James Bible is the perfect, preserved Word of God for the English-speaking world. This is a big deal to me because I know many men who are not fundamentalists and believe that the King James Bible came from the right manuscripts. Many take that position because it is more acceptable with their scholarly friends. I want to be around the crowd that cares what the Spirit of God thinks. I want that leather-lung, old-time religion. I am not interested in anything evangelical. I do not want anything that even looks evangelical around me.

> *There is nothing that shapes our character more than the people with whom we choose to spend our time.*

I will not allow men to preach in my church who are teachers only. I like teaching, but I like red-hot, gun barrel-straight, leather-lung, let-her-rip preaching better! I do not want to be around a man who does not clear off a spot every few services to throw a fit. There is a ministerial culture that promotes teaching only. When you start reading the evangelical books about how to build the super churches, you start trying to make sure you get the rough edges off. I do not want one rough edge off of me! I want folks to get every splinter they can get when they sit on the old pine benches! We do not need anything new – we need it old. I use the word "old" every chance I get. We need the old-time religion again in our country. I am leery of anyone who is trying to shift away from even the words "old fashioned."

There are three or four great fundamental preachers who, ten years ago, were my heroes but are now drifting toward evangelicalism because of whom they are running with. They have been around those who talk about "paradigm shifts" and being "seeker sensitive." I do not know what those things mean. I like sinners, the Bible, old-time religion, and preaching against sin. If a guy with a sixth grade education cannot understand it, I do not want it!

Do you evaluate your friendships? Are they drawing you away from Christ, or are they drawing you toward Christ? Are they pulling you away from spirituality or pushing you toward spirituality? Are there any Delilahs in your life that you need to deal with, child of God?

2. *The Force Of Samson's Temptation.*

"And Delilah said to Samson, Tell me, I pray thee, wherein thy great strength lieth, and wherewith thou mightest be bound to afflict thee" (Judges 16:6). Satan does not give up easily. He went after our Saviour with three shots; he went after Samson with four. You can guarantee that he is not going to give up easily on you either. Verse 16 says, *"And it came to pass, when she pressed him daily with her words, and urged him, so that his soul was vexed unto death."* Delilah would not back down or let up.

A. *When We Give In Gradually, We Will Give In Eventually.*

It is vital that we figure out what the Bible teaches is right and draw a line. We then must not cross the line. We must believe that even just one step across the line can result in tragedy. Even a small compromise should make us feel dirty, when, in reality, we are probably more right than ninety-five percent of the Christians in America. If you make your line straight with the Bible as the rule, even if you fall a little bit, you will be okay.

I love home-school families, but there are dangers in the home-school movement like there are dangers in every movement. Some in the home-school movement have gone so far that they believe in home church as well. They call churches like ours segregated churches, meaning that we segregate the children from their parents. Of course we believe in children's classes, not only for specialized teaching, but also so that the parents can teach Sunday school and serve God. I saw a service on video where the children were with their parents in the service, and it was the biggest bunch of horse hockey and tomfoolery you have ever seen in your life. There were kids screaming and people interrupting. If somebody walked in and saw that, they would think that the church was a cult.

> *When we give in Gradually, we will give in Eventually.*

I understand that by putting your family in a church, someone in that church could hurt your family. I understand the fear that a home-school family faces while trying to guard their children from the wrong influences. However, you have to draw the line on what you believe about the church. If God said that we are not to forsake the assembling of ourselves together, then that is a line you have to draw. It does not matter how good you are in your home-school conviction, if someone tries to pull you over, say, "We are not crossing that line."

I have a good preacher friend that drew a line he refused to cross. A lady who often came to his church played the lottery regularly. She won the inter-state lottery and received a check for eighty-seven million dollars. She went by the preacher's office one day and handed him a check for 8.7 million dollars, the tithe from her lottery winnings. He ripped up the check in front of her and said, "We are not going to build anything around here and have this community say, 'That is the church that the lottery built.'" She got offended and left. His church is giving nearly half a million dollars to missions right now and doing just fine. This dear brother drew a line and didn't cross it.

You must draw a line. Inevitably, someone will tempt you someday. That temptation will feel right at the moment, and, if a line is not drawn, you will yield to the temptation. You must decide what you believe.

Let me address young people. Do not leave your church and live like the heathen and then say, "Well, those convictions that the preacher preached were never mine personally." Sit down with the preacher and have him show you the Bible on why he preaches and believes what he does. When you go out and live like a fool, what Bible are you going to use to justify your actions? Draw a line.

Girls, your parents and leaders remember when you were a baby. To them, you are still just a little girl, but some of the boys in your church think you are the most gorgeous thing they have ever set eyes on! Some of the boys will begin to be interested in you, and that is okay. We want them to be interested in the girls, not each other! I double-dog dare every girl to make up her mind that she is too pretty and valuable to sell out to anybody. If some boy tries to kiss you say, "You know, I'd like to, but you don't look like my dad, and he is the only man I have ever kissed. If you want to proceed with this, you can pucker, but you will not get what you are expecting! You are going to get four fingers halfway down your throat! As you swallow teeth, remember that you ran into a real lady that is not for sale." They might laugh at you, but it sure would be awesome if the rumor spread throughout the school that the boy missing three teeth was the one who tried to mess with you! I can guarantee that you would be respected; your stock would shoot through the roof! Folks would say, "That is a real lady." I dare you girls to draw a line.

You will end up with the best man possible if you draw the line. If you are insecure and afraid that you will never get a man, you would be better off being an old maid than getting the wrong one. If you spend four years in college and get a degree but do not get a husband, it will be okay. It is better than marrying the wrong one. I know some girls who thought they got the right one in Bible college but did not feel so good about it later when their husband left them for another woman.

If I were a girl, I would look for a man with character. You will know he has character if he does not have much time to spend with you. If he is working a job and going to college, and he can flirt with you three or four nights a week, you have a deadbeat on your hands. Ask him, "Did you read your Bible today? You mean that you want to talk to me, and you have not read your Bible yet? How am I going to know that you are not a charlatan and a fraud?" Ask him to read his Bible with you, and you will really know if he knows the Author of it. You will be reading along, and he will say, "This command is why you and I can't kiss until we get married." If he reads past those verses quickly, you say, "Wait a minute! Time out! Stop! Explain your position on this verse because it is how you are going to raise my daughters. I want to know which convictions you will use to raise them."

B. When We Toy With Temptation, Temptation Traps Us.

Ralph Emerson says, "Call on God, but row away from the rocks." Are there things in your life that you need to deal with in a drastic way? Perhaps the following changes need to take place in your life:

➢ **Get Rid Of The Internet.** You may have to sit down with your family after reading a book like this and say, "I am sorry. Dad has been wrong. We have to straighten some things up. We are getting rid of the Internet access we have in our house. Dad thought he needed it, but now he realizes that he is setting you up for a fall, and I love you too much to destroy you or to have any part in your destruction."

➢ **Firm Up Your Convictions.**

➢ **Revamp Your Lifestyle.**

➢ **Eliminate Unhealthy Leisure Activities.**

➢ **Reconsider Employment.** You may think that God gave you the job you have, but He did not give it to you if it is going to destroy you. You would be better off to take a pay cut, move into a smaller house, drive an older car, and be happily married than to struggle with temptation every day of your married life not knowing if you are going to make it.

Fleeing is hard, but sometimes it is essential. The Bible says to flee youthful lusts and fornication.

THE DEGRADATION SAMSON FELT

And she said, The Philistines be upon thee, Samson. And he awoke out of his sleep, and said, I will go out as at other times before, and shake myself. And he wist not that the LORD was departed from him. But the Philistines took him, and put out his eyes, and brought him down to Gaza, and bound him with fetters of brass; and he did grind in the prison house. **Judges 16:20-21**

The Philistines had never taken Samson before. They had fought him and battled him but never taken him. The mighty Samson was no longer able to stop their assault; he was just like any other man. Although called by God to judge Israel and endued with mighty power to accomplish the work that God had called him to do, Samson ended his life in captivity to his enemies. When Samson gave in to his temptation, it cost him three things:

> *"Call on God, but row away from the rocks."*
>
> ~ Ralph Waldo Emerson

1. Samson Lost His Strength.

The mighty man who had walked off with the gates of Gaza in an amazing display of physical strength was now bound. He was reduced to doing the physical work of a slave in chains. Do you remember when you were strong for God? Do you remember when the glow in your heart caused you to think that *you* were an over-comer? Have you lost your spiritual strength, Samson, because of self-indulgence? Do you not have the strength to pray or to go soul winning or to say no to your passions?

2. Samson Lost His Sight.

Have you ever tried to picture the day the Philistines removed Samson's eyes? The culture of the Philistines would have been to sear Samson's eyes with a hot iron. Can you imagine as they took a red-hot poker and stuck it in the eye sockets of Israel's champion? Can you hear that great warrior – and that man who had killed one thousand Philistines with the jawbone of and ass- scream? Can you imagine the agony he suffered? Can you see the Philistines around him laughing? His vision was gone. He was as blind as the beggars Jesus met by the wayside.

Does this explain why some of us as believers have lost our spiritual sight? The Word of God no longer flashes with new meaning to us. We are blind to a lost world. We are not involved in the work of evangelism. We no longer see men slipping off into hell! The dangers people are facing do not even seem to register on our radar anymore. Child of God, has the devil taken your vision away? Has he taken your vision for raising a great family? Has he taken your vision for having a model marriage?

3. Samson Lost His Service.

Samson could no longer serve God as a true Nazarite. Instead, he was doing the job of a donkey at a gristmill. The yoke he was pushing was reserved for a donkey, a beast of burden. Is there any more pitiful picture in the Bible of unbridled passions reducing a man of great potential? His eyes were scarred beyond imaginable thought, and he was doing the job of a donkey.

There was a man who was a bus director of a great church, but he did not deal with some things. He thought he could hide his "secret" life, but he got caught. His secret life was serious enough to cost him fifteen years in the state penitentiary. He ended up in a halfway house riding a van to church. He sat in the front row and dreamed of the days he had spoken in national bus conferences as a leader in our country. He dreamed of the days he had brought boys and girls to Sunday school.

He went to his preacher and said, "Preacher, could God ever use me again."

His preacher said, "Well, God could never use you in the bus ministry again, but you could work in our parking lot."

I wonder if every time that man parks a bus he remembers the day he led a bus ministry. The pleasure is just not worth it, child of God. You are going to get caught. You are not the exception. You either deal with your temptation, or your temptation will deal with you. You either ***Toy With It And Tumble***, or you ***Resist It And Rumble***!

The last part of Judges 16:21 says, "A*nd he did grind in the prison house."* That word *grind* is an interesting word. Is that what God's service has become to you – a grind? Deacon, has your office become a grind to you? Do you enjoy it today as much as you did the day you were elected? Has your Sunday school class become a grind, teacher? If you teach sixth grade boys, you are responsible for every sixth grade boy that lives in your area. Do not be content with five or six pupils. You are just going through the motions because it has become a grind. You might say, "Well, I am just going to quit! I have too much on my plate."

Quitting is not the answer. You might need to quit *something*, but you do not need to quit serving God. You need to quit toying with the temptation that is taking all of your spiritual energy. How about your bus route? How about your nursery ministry? How about your choir work? How about your ushering? How about your ministry, staff member? How about your studies, college student? Are you just grinding with no motivation or joy?

> *You either deal with your temptation, or your temptation will deal with you.*

page • 165

6

THE PROBLEM EXPERIENCED

The struggle with the flesh is the heart of the problem.

O wretched man that I am! who shall deliver me from the body of this death? I thank my God through Jesus Christ our Lord. **Romans 7:24-25a**

This chapter is going to deal with the most common words we ever utter in this arena of temptation. Those words are: "Why did I do that again?" No matter how long we have been saved, no matter how wrong we know it is, not matter how much we do not want to do it, we cry, "Why did I do it again?"

Have you ever said those words to yourself? Have you ever wondered why you fall again and again? Perhaps you heard a preacher mention " besetting sins," and you thought, "That's it! That's my problem!" But then it really got you down when you began to think that you had more than one besetting sin. The Bible says *"besetting **sin**"* not **sins**. You do *not* have many besetting sins, but it seems like you do because you have created a pattern that needs to be stopped. When the devil knows you are easy prey in one arena, he will begin to attack you in several arenas. Before long, you are a basket case thinking about suicide. You do not even know if life is worth living. Then you start wondering if the Bible is true, because you wonder how the Bible could be true while you are so messed up.

Even though a man is saved, there is a **Part** of him that did not get saved. There is a **Part** of man that does not get to cross the divide and go to heaven. That part is the body, wherein lies the old nature, or the flesh. Paul's words in Romans 7:15-25 contain the believers struggle with his flesh. He said that the part of him that was not saved by redemption was absolutely untrustworthy. *"For I know that in me (that is, in my flesh,) dwelleth no good thing."*

I heard a sermon years ago entitled, "There is no Such Thing as Spiritual Pride." The preacher was riding his point longer than my flesh wanted to hear. He went so far as to say that it is never right to say that you are proud of anything associated with yourself. Especially, we should not say that we are proud of our children. It is not wrong to praise our children, but we as parents should not take pride in our children. If your children turn out right, it has been or will be *In Spite* of you, not *Because Of* you.

> *It is not wrong to praise our children, but we as parents should not take pride in our children.*

Some folks do not like that kind of teaching. Is it wrong to be proud of your accomplishments? Well, what have you

page • 168

accomplished that you did not need God's help to accomplish? We need to be careful about being proud of anything because the *New Nature* is never proud. Pride is in the domain of the **Old Nature.** Paul said that nothing about the old nature is praiseworthy. Nothing in the old nature is good.

Paul states in Romans 7:21, "*I find then a law, that, when I would do good, evil is present with me.*" He was referring to authority. If I walked into your house and said, "Hold it up in the name of the law!" I would be saying that I had authority to give instructions or take dominion. When Paul is talking about these two laws, he is saying that there are two authorities trying to govern me.

One of the most frustrating things for the child of God is the *spiritual struggle* in which he finds himself on a *daily basis.* The struggle will not go away. It does not matter how separated you get or how spiritual you are, you will not outrun temptation. You had better learn how to battle it, because you will never completely beat it as long as you have your old nature.

You are not alone in experiencing these frustrating feelings. The Apostle Paul felt the same way, and he gave us some insight into those feelings in Romans 7:15-25. I not only want to *feel good*, but I also want some *victory*! Paul gave us some instructions on how to live victoriously.

The Perplexing Situation Of The Believer

For we know that the law is spiritual: but I am carnal, sold under sin. **Romans 7:14**

When Adam sinned, mankind was "*sold under sin.*" Just as the slave is sold and does his master's will above his own, so we are slaves to sin because we were conceived in iniquity and born in sin. Paul's old nature was what kept him in check when he wanted to soar upward.

The **New Nature** cannot commit sin. The **Old Nature** cannot do anything but sin. The reason you will not deal with your flesh more ferociously is because you do not believe that the **Old Nature** is incapable of doing good. It is also the reason you **Pacify Your Flesh** instead of **Crucifying Your Flesh**. It is also the reason you **Corral Your Flesh** instead of **Condemning Your Flesh**. Why would you corral a rattlesnake? You may be an environmentalist that loves rattlesnakes, but I do not. If there is a rattlesnake living under my porch, one of us is going to move! I am not going to live with that danger lurking in my world. Child of God, every day that you pacify your flesh, you are living with a rattlesnake!

"Whosoever is born of God doth not commit sin; for his seed remaineth in him: and he cannot sin, because he is born of God" (I John 3:9). If this verse does not mean that your new nature cannot commit sin, then it means that people who are saved cannot commit sin. If that is the case, then none of us are saved! It does

not mean that a saved person is incapable of sin; it means that your *New Nature* is incapable of sin.

The *Old Nature* cannot do right because it has not been born of God; it has been born of Adam. The *Old Nature* has been born of the devil; hence, it cannot perform anything **Righteous**, although it can perform that which is **Religious**. The old nature can teach Sunday school, but it cannot make a difference. The old nature can preach, but it cannot change anybody's life. Matthew 7:22-23 says, *"Many will say to me in that day, Lord, Lord, have we not prophesied in thy name? and in thy name have cast out devils? and in thy name done many wonderful works? And then will I profess unto them, I never knew you: depart from me, ye that work iniquity."*

The *Old Nature* can do religious things, but it just cannot change anybody's life.

I *have* to win the battle over the devil! Victory is not optional! There are two certainties in the life of the believer because of our two natures:

1. An Obvious Desire To Do Right

One of the ways you know you are saved is that you have an obvious desire to do right that you never had before. *"For that which I do I allow not: for **what I would**, that do I not; but what I hate, that do I"* (Romans 7:15). Paul wanted to do what was right, even though he did wrong. He stated *"For I know that in me (that is, in my flesh,) dwelleth no good thing: for to will is* *present with me; but how to perform that which is good I find not. For the good that I would I do not: but the evil which I would not, that I do."* (Romans 7:18-19)

Paul had the best of intentions. He had a strong resolve, but he kept stumbling and falling. I am not worried about the one who wants to do right but keeps falling; I am worried about the one who has no will to do right. You can sin and be saved; you just cannot have as much fun at sinning as some folks are having.

"I find then a law, that, when I would do good, evil is present with me. For I delight in the law of God after the inward man" (Romans 7:21-22). Paul was saying that there was a part of him that found great delight in the law of God. I would rather hear that you are struggling with having a desire to listen to country music than to hear that you are not interested in the things of God at all. I was on my way to New Hampshire with my son at 4:00 A.M. We turned on our church's radio station, and Brother Mays Jackson was preaching. My soul! Brother Mays blessed our hearts. You may struggle and fall, but you should rejoice that there is a part of you that likes the things of God. The folks that do not have any hunger for the things of God worry me.

> *I am not worried about the one who wants to do right but keeps falling; I am worried about the one who has no will to do right.*

A Delaware Indian Chief was sitting at the fireside of a friend. Both of them were looking silently at the fire, indulging their own reflections. At

page • 172

length, the silence was broken by the friend, who said, "I will tell thee what I have been thinking of. I have been thinking of a rule delivered by the Author of the Christian religion which, from its excellence, we call the 'Golden Rule'."

The Chief raised his hand and said, "Stop! Don't praise it to me, but rather tell me what it is, and let me think for myself. I do not wish you to tell me of its excellence. Tell me what it is."

The friend replied, "It is for one man to do to another as he would have the other do to him."

As soon as the Chief of the Delaware heard his friend describe the "Golden Rule," he said, "It is impossible! It cannot be done."

Silence again ensued. In about a quarter of an hour, he came to his friend with a smiling countenance and said, "Brother, I have been thoughtful of what you told me. If the Great Spirit that made man would give him a new heart, he could do as you say, but not else."

Thus, the Indian chief identified the only means by which man can fulfill the "Golden Rule." The "Great Spirit" has to give you a new heart. The flesh has no desire to do or act right. However, if the Holy Spirit inhabits a life, there will be a desire to follow His leading. This desire is one of the purest indications of salvation. I Peter 2:2 states, *"As newborn babes, desire the sincere milk of the word, that ye may grow thereby."* You do not have to teach a baby to want milk; that desire is inborn. Likewise, a Christian does not have to be taught to attend church; that desire is inborn. I do not think that you have to argue with somebody who is saved about being baptized. You may have to explain it to him and give a little grace for God to reveal it to him, but you will not have to argue with him. Evangelist Joe Boyd said, "If they won't get wet, they never got dipped in the blood!" A man that will not get wet for Jesus was probably never redeemed by Jesus. The desire is part of the new nature that God puts in a man when He saves him.

> *If we are truly born again, our inward man will have a delight in knowing and doing and submitting to the will of God.*

If we are truly born again, our inward man will have a delight in knowing and doing and submitting to the will of God. We will never be happier than when we are living in accordance with the Bible. Although the ***Flesh*** of the believer may delight in ***Rebelling Against The Law Of God***, the ***Mind*** of the believer will truly ***Delight In Obedience Toward The Law Of God***.

2. An Overwhelming Departure From Doing Right.

> *For that which I do I allow not: for what I would, that do I not; but what I hate, that do I. If then I do that which I would not, I consent unto the law that it is good. For the good that I would I do not: but the evil which I would not, that I do.* **Romans 7:15-16, 19**

Paul said, "I may have an obvious desire to do right, but at the same time there is, in my heart, an overwhelming departure from doing right." Can you identify with Paul? Paul desired to do the good and avoid the bad, but he discovered, to his utter frustration, that he was doing the bad and avoiding the good. You might say that Paul was long on Desire but short on Determination. There was a will, but there was no way.

So it is with the child of God. Many false doctrines have been fostered because of this struggle. The Armenian brethren have said that if a man cannot win the battle with temptation then he is not saved. I understand why they drifted that way, though I am not in agreement with them. They were frustrated with the battle. John Wesley, a proponent of the Armenian doctrine, said on his deathbed, "I have yet to achieve complete sanctification."

There is another crowd that says that since the desire to do wrong is within us, God put it there. Consequently, it does not matter how one lives as long as he shouts and praises Jesus. That is called the doctrine of license, and it is just as wrong as the doctrine that teaches that you can lose your salvation.

We are faced with a perplexing situation. We have a *New Nature* that only has a desire to do the things that are holy, godly, and righteous; and we have an *Old Nature* that has an interest solely in departing from the things that are holy, godly, and righteous. The unavoidable battle does not mean that victory is not achievable and defeat is inevitable. If you give in to the *Old Nature*, you will only enjoy the pleasures of your sin for a season. They are temporary. However, the joys of resisting Satan will last eternally!

It brings me great joy when the devil has tempted, thwarted, and tricked me, and I am still standing at the end of the day! He may have gotten me close to defeat, but somehow, someway, God prevailed and strength came. I may lose tomorrow, but I at least have one day to say, "I whipped you, old devil!" The secret to a happy life is amassing more and more of those days of victory.

A funeral director was shocked by an occurrence in his funeral parlor. A wicked woman had died. A short time before the funeral was to be conducted, another worldly woman, the sister of the dead woman, came in and placed a set of dice in one hand of her deceased sister and a pack of cigarettes in the other hand. The undertaker was puzzled and asked the woman what she was doing.

She said, "I thought my sister might want to shoot dice and smoke in the other world."

Being a Christian, the funeral director replied, "Well, she may desire to do those things, but that desire will never be gratified because the Bible says in Revelation 18:14, *'And the fruits that thy soul lusted after are departed from thee . . . and thou shalt find them no more at all'.*"

There is coming a day when your **Old Nature** will never find that for which it is searching. Since the day is coming, you might as well start denying your flesh now! Denying your flesh is a good feeling. Some of us have lived so long doing whatever the flesh desires, that we cannot imagine resisting it. If you had experienced the joy on the other side of resisting, then you would feel differently.

I have messed up. I look back on twenty-five years of being saved, and see many failures. I have often charted a course for victory and ended up in defeat. Oh, but I want to tell you that the days that I get to bed late, worn out because the devil has tempted and tried me without success make me feel good about the struggle in which I am engaged.

The Powerful Struggle In The Believer

For I know that in me (that is, in my flesh,) dwelleth no good thing: for to will is present with me; but how to perform that which is good I find not. **Romans 7:18**

Paul was literally saying that he had an earnest and intense desire to find the way to victory. Overcoming our fleshly desires is a daily battle. Satan may have lost us because we are saved, but he has not left us! John Phillips described it this way: Suppose a biologist were to perform an experiment by grafting, at a given stage of development, a beautiful butterfly with a black widow spider in such a way that the two creatures were fused into one and thus grew to maturity. What a clash of instincts there would be in a monstrosity like this! One part of the creature's nature would long for the clear skies of heaven, while the other part would crave a web in a dark corner and a diet of blood. What could be done with such a horrendous creature? Nothing, except to put it to death.

> ***Overcoming our fleshly desires is a daily battle.***

In some sense, that is precisely what happened in the Garden of Eden. Satan performed a diabolical surgery in which he turned the human race into a two-headed monster. One side is the lovely butterfly that tries to reach the heavens; the other side is a dark, sinister, evil nature that feeds off the blood of others. Look at two observations of that sinful nature:

1. The Presence Of The Sinful Nature.

> *Now if I do that I would not, it is no more I that do it, but sin that dwelleth in me. I find then a law, that, when I would do good, evil is present with me. For I delight in the law of God after the inward man: But I see another law in my members, warring against the law of my mind, and bringing me into captivity to the law of sin which is in my members.* **Romans 7:20-23**

We have an ***Old Nature*** that is in us and with us every day. The presence of this ***Old Nature*** makes separated living a very important necessity in winning the battle over temptation. However, separation alone will not fix the problem. Though you may separate from dirty, filthy, immoral, ungodly things, you still have to deal with the nature that desires those things. Because it is harder to get the ungodly things if you cannot find them, separation is a good thing. For this reason, you need to re-evaluate your need for cable TV in your home. You also need to pray about whether or not it is God's will for you to have Internet in your home. Having cable TV and Internet access in your home gives your

Old Nature easy access to whatever tempts you. I was talking to a Christian the other day who told me that his besetting sin was playing Internet poker. He said that he only played with fifteen or twenty dollars, but he just loved it. Playing Internet poker is his besetting sin. The reason you battle with your besetting sin is because you have an evil nature that **enjoys** it.

The corruption of the ***Old Nature*** causes a daily inclination toward sin. The new nature hates this tendency to sin. The new nature fights against it and

Though you may separate from dirty, filthy, immoral, ungodly things, you still have to deal with the nature that desires those things.

resists its efforts to control our lives, yet Galatians 5:17 says, *"For the flesh lusteth against the Spirit, and the Spirit against the flesh: and these are contrary the one to the other: so that ye cannot do the things that ye would."* This struggle between the flesh and the Spirit is a powerful struggle because of the presence of our evil nature. Satan's goal is long-term, meaning that it does not matter to him if he completely defeats us in one day or not. You may have a shortsighted plan, but Satan sees the whole picture. His goal is to destroy us one step, one yielding, one stumble at a time until he destroys our effectiveness for Christ.

I talked to a Christian not long ago who has battled with specific temptations for years. This was a fairly young person, yet he had battles that would scare you. His temptations had been long and deep and deviant. This young Christian with great potential said to me, "I am thinking about suicide. I am wicked and ungodly, and there is no hope for me. I can't win. In fact, this whole scenario almost makes me want to believe in Calvinism. Maybe I was predestined to be this way." I said, "Time out! Now the devil has so warped you that he is confusing your doctrine."

This very same confusion influenced Charles Taze Russell, a Congregational Sunday school teacher. Because of unresolved battles in his life, he decided that he did not believe there was a Hell. Before long, he did not even believe there was a trinity. He became the founder of the Jehovah's Witnesses. The hell-damning doctrine of the Jehovah's Witnesses came from a man who could not deal with the struggle of temptation and could not realize what the devil and God were doing. If you allow the devil to continue to mess with you, some things that now seem unbelievable will become possible.

2. The Power Of The Sinful Nature.

> *But I see another law in my members, warring against the law of my mind, and **bringing me into captivity** to the law of sin which is in my members.* **Romans 7:23**

We are not fighting an ordinary foe. Satan has plenty of experience in this arena of temptation, and he will use every tactic necessary to accomplish his goals. This ***Sinful Nature*** has the **Power to Imprison Us Within the Walls of Our Own Actions and Our Own Imaginations**. We look free, but we are literally addicted and imprisoned to our passions. I talk with people all the time who describe what should be unthinkable as the real, normal world in which they live.

An old Indian was once asked to describe something about his salvation. Having been saved a short time, he did not know the theological terms with which to answer. In his simplicity, he described two dogs fighting within him on a constant basis. When asked which dog was winning today, he replied, "The one I fed the most yesterday."

We have seen the ***Perplexing Situation Of The Believer***, and the ***Powerful Struggle In The Believer***, but there is a final certainty in Romans chapter seven.

The Proposed Solution For The Believer

O wretched man that I am! who shall deliver me from the body of this death? I thank God through Jesus Christ our Lord. So then with the mind I myself serve the law of God; but with the flesh the law of sin. **Romans 7:24-25**

If the Scriptures only informed us of the struggle within and its inherent frustration, how miserable life would be! I am thrilled to report that Paul did not stop with that thought! Paul gives the answer. We are not left without hope in our struggle! Paul found a solution by realizing some truths about himself:

1. He Realized The Plight Of A Sinful Man.

O wretched man that I am! *who shall deliver me from the body of this death?* **Romans 7:24**

You cannot do anything about the fact that you were born a sinner. Whether you have been saved for three days or three decades, you are a still a sinner saved by grace. You will never have victory, or even understand that the battle can be won, if you do not come to the realization of the plight of a sinful man. Notice in verse 24 that Paul refers to himself as a wretched man. In his own account, Paul stated that he was wretched and hopeless. He stated that he was corrupt in his nature, which was why he was not as good as he wanted to be. Paul realized that **he** could not control, change, or conquer the flesh. Flesh will not kill flesh.

We will never embark on the road to victory until we are willing to admit our sinful state. That is why the songwriter penned the words, *"It's me, it's me, it's me, O Lord, standin' in the need of prayer. Not my mother, not my brother, but it's me, O Lord, standin' in the need of prayer."* The biggest impediment to victory is pride. Pride is the reason that some people will not get counsel from a pastor, a more mature Christian, or even a program like Reformers Unanimous. They will not admit the fact that they have

> *We will never embark on the road to victory until we are willing to admit our sinful state.*

no more victory than a skid row drunkard. The fact that you are cleaned up and look better than a drunkard on the outside does not mean that the passions in your world are not as wicked and controlling as his. A drinking problem is an obvious problem while pride is a hidden problem. I am not sure what is worse – an obvious problem or a hidden problem.

2. He Realized The Power Of A Serving Mind.

I thank God through Jesus Christ our Lord. So then **with the mind I myself serve the law of God;** *but with the flesh the law of sin.* **Romans 7:25**

The battle is won or lost in the mind. Paul realized the power of the mind as he spoke these words in Philippians 2:5, *"Let this mind be in you, which was also in Christ Jesus,"* and also, *"And be not conformed to this world: but be ye transformed by the renewing of your mind, that ye may prove what is that good, and acceptable,*

> *What you see and hear determines what you think about, and what you think about ultimately determines what you do.*

and perfect, will of God," Romans 12:2. It is a law of nature that what you see and hear determines what you think about, and what you think about ultimately determines what you do. Proverbs 23:7 states, *"For as he thinketh in his heart, so is he."* You cannot control it. If you sit for two hours in front of a bunch

page • 183

of heathens and perverts who are cussing on the television screen, you will say the same words when your anger gets riled up. Those words come from the filth on which your mind has been feeding. Matthew 12:34 says, *"O generation of vipers, how can ye, being evil, speak good things? for **out of the abundance of the heart the mouth speaketh.**"*

My wife and I had been married just a few months when my in-laws took us to Hershey Park, Pennsylvania to an amusement park at the headquarters of Hershey Chocolate Company. We rode on roller coasters and had a fun day. On the edge of the park, there was a dome-shaped building. When I enquired about it, everybody told me that I did not want to go in there because it was the most petrifying ride in the park. My brother-in-law said, "If you go in there, you'll get sick. I get sick every time I go in there." Being the fool that I am, I said, "That sounds like a dare." So I went in there all alone.

There was a concrete floor with a row of bars every four feet. When I got in there, the personnel said to hold onto the bars. I thought they were crazy, so I did not hold onto the bar. It was a 3-D theater. When the movie started, we were on a plane that was banking into the Grand Canyon. Everybody around me was screaming, and I thought they were all stupid. Then we were on a roller coaster. Once again, the people in front of me were screaming. Somewhere between the plane ride in the Grand Canyon and the roller coaster ride, I forgot where I was. We banked into one curve, and I said, "Oh, man! We're going to die!" When I came out of the ride, my family said, "How was it?" Of course, I said, "There was nothing to it." I was not going to admit to my brother-in-law that he was right.

In that goofy experiment that day I learned the law of nature. I did not conquer that ride. I closed my eyes because I found that when my eyes were closed the banks and turns did not scare me. Men, you cannot look at that dirty picture in the break room. Get those tool posters out of your garage. Ladies, do not believe that your husband is just a tool guy – he is struggling, and he does not need any help to continue to do so.

For years now, when any catalog has come into our home, my wife has ripped out about fifteen pages. It may seem crazy, but I do not need to look at women in underclothing. If you have your wife conned in this area, I hope I am peeling back the veneer. If you look at that kind of thing, it will get progressively worse, and before long it will be full-fledged pornography. If you keep messing around in that world, before long you will be doing things that are unthinkable. You may even end up in jail for the ungodly, perverted things you are capable of doing if you feed on that junk. You had better stop the train before it comes to its own disastrous end.

Fanny Crosby wrote over 9,000 hymns during her lifetime. Nine thousand hymns would fill seventeen average hymn books. She was born healthy, but at six weeks of age, she had an eye infection, which a quack doctor treated by placing hot poultices on her red, inflamed eyelids. The infection did clear up, but scars formed on the eyes as a result of the hot poultices, blinding the baby girl for life. She was not blind because she had to be; she was blind as the result of malpractice.

If you know Fanny Crosby's testimony, you know that a bitter word never escaped her lips. In fact, one day a preacher said to her, "Fanny, I feel so sorry for you. I wish you could see."

She said, "If I could have but one prayer request, my request would be for God to make me blind again because my blindness has enabled me to see what others cannot see. Do not deprive me of the pleasure of having my Lord and Savior be the first thing these eyes ever behold."

Two months after she went blind, her father died. Her twenty-one year old mother, Mercy Crosby, was left alone with a blind baby. If she had been a twenty-first century woman, she would have gone into depression, committed suicide, and killed the baby. In reality, she did not know that depression was an option, so she hired herself out as a maid while grandmother, Eunice Crosby, took care of little Fanny. Grandmother took the education of her little granddaughter upon herself and became the little girl's eyes, vividly describing the physical world. Grandmother's careful teaching helped develop Fanny's descriptive abilities. She also nurtured Fanny's spirit. She forbade Fanny to feel sorry for herself. She would not allow her to become a victim of her blindness. She taught her that her blindness was not a curse but a blessing. Fanny grew up understanding that she had no right to complain.

Mrs. Hawley, a landlady of the Crosby's, was probably the second greatest influence in Fanny's life. She taught Fanny the Bible. Fanny Crosby left home at age fifteen to go to the New York Institute of the Blind and never returned again. Mrs. Hawley set a goal to help Fanny memorize five chapters of the Bible per week. By the time she was fifteen years of age, she had memorized the entire Pentateuch – she could quote Genesis, Exodus, Leviticus, Numbers, and Deuteronomy in one sitting. She had also memorized all of the Gospels, the Proverbs, the Song of Solomon, and nearly the entire book of Psalms. Those books together contain over 13,000 Bible verses and 300,000 Bible words. Jesus said, *"Man shall not live by bread alone, but by every word that proceedeth out of the mouth of God"* (Matthew 4:4). Fanny Crosby could quote 13,000 Bible verses. No wonder 9,000 Gospel hymns came out of her life.

> *So much good came out of Fanny Crosby's life because so much good went into her life.*

We are so shallow that there is nothing to us. Instead of young preacher boys reading the Bible, they are playing Sony PlayStation. We have not reared a generation that knows God. Our kids know the television dial better than they know the Bible. They know where the channels are, but they do not know how to quote the books of the Bible. How can we wonder why we are rearing perverts? We can blame it on the Christian school or the youth group, but the problem lies with mom and dad not understanding that it is their job to train up the next generation.

Fanny Crosby wrote the words, "Blessed assurance, Jesus is mine," along with the following songs and many others:

"All the Way My Savior Leads Me"
"To God Be the Glory"
"Pass Me Not, O Gentle Savior"

"Safe in the Arms of Jesus"
"Rescue the Perishing"
"Jesus, Keep Me Near the Cross"
"I Am Thine, O Lord"
"He Hideth My Soul"
"My Savior First of All"
"Praise Him, Praise Him"
"Redeemed How I Love to Proclaim It"
"There's Room at the Cross for You"
"There Shall Be Showers of Blessing"
"Tell Me the Story of Jesus"

Allow me to reiterate the fact that so much good came out of Fanny Crosby's life because so much good went in. We battle with temptation because we are shallow. The reason that men cannot conquer passion, lust, and sin is because they do not have enough power in their will and nature to memorize and meditate on the Bible instead of the Internet.

Fanny Crosby lived to be ninety-five. For the last fifteen years of her life, she devoted several nights a week of service as an altar worker in the local rescue mission. She just loved to take the Gospel to sinners. It was not unusual to see her sitting next to some old drunkard.

She would say to him, "Son, you have a momma, don't you, boy? What's your momma's name? Where is she tonight?" Often, before she finished speaking, the man would be weeping. She would continue, "Son, your momma is probably praying that you will get saved. She probably never wanted you to turn out like this. Let's go down to the altar and answer momma's prayer tonight."

I do not wish blindness on our children, but I do wonder what God could do with them. I wonder what demons they may have to face. I wonder what generational curses we could bring to a screeching halt if we would be concerned with more than just whether they received an "A" in school or scored a basket. I wonder what could happen if we worried about whether or not they knew the God of the Bible.

One of Fanny Crosby's last hymns was "My Savior First of All":

When my life's work is ended and I cross the swelling tide,
When the bright and glorious morning I shall see,
I shall know my Redeemer when I reach the other side,
And His smile will be the first to welcome me.

I shall know Him, I shall know Him,
And redeemed by His side I shall stand,
I shall know Him, I shall know Him
By the print of the nails in His hand.

Fanny Crosby was assured that she would know Jesus when she saw Him because she already knew Him!

We will never win the battle over temptation if we do not first realize the **Plight Of A Sinful Man** and secondly, the **Power Of A Serving Mind**. Your mind will serve something, and whatever it serves will become a very powerful force in your life. Make up your mind that you are going to serve God in order to please Him.

Get so involved in the things of God that there is no way out.

3. He Realized The Power Of A Strengthening Master.

> *I thank God through Jesus Christ our Lord. So then with the mind I myself serve the law of God; but with the flesh the law of sin.* **Romans 7:25**

> *Now unto him that is able to keep you from falling, and to present you faultless before the presence of his glory with exceeding joy.* **Jude 24**

Everybody that is saved and sincere wants to be freed from sin, but we cannot succeed when we do not understand how to be freed. You do not get freed from sin; you find another Master! Who is your master? Is your master the Lord Jesus Christ, the Spirit of the living God? Or is your master your passions, feelings, emotions, will, or desire to do right? Everything you have must be submitted to the Lordship of Jesus Christ. You will never be freed from sin; you have to get a new Master.

Years ago, the picture *Freedom versus Bondage* was painted, depicting a chess game in which the devil had moved his queen and had a young man in checkmate. Many who knew chess well and had studied the picture agreed that the depiction was correct and that the young man had no recourse but defeat. It had even become a form of entertainment for folks to look at the picture to see if there was a mistake in the painting. A retired, undefeated chess champion by the name of Paul Murphy was summoned to look at the picture. After about thirty minutes, his face broke into a smile, and he said, "Young man, make that move! And then make that move." For years, many different people had been confident that the young man in the picture had been put in an impossible situation by the devil, but they were wrong.

> *You will never be freed from your sin; you will have to get another Master.*

There have been times in my world when it seemed the devil had me in checkmate and my only option was to go down in defeat. The devil has said, "You might as well just be a heathen. You might as well quit church. You might as well be an evangelical. There is no reason to be an old-time Christian. You are defeated." Then it seemed as if the blessed Holy Spirit of God whispered to my heart, "Move here, young man. Move there, young man!" When I made the move, I found out that *"God is faithful, who will not suffer you to be tempted above that ye are able; but will with the temptation also make a way to escape, that ye may be able to bear it"* I Corinthians 10:13.

You will never be freed from your sin; you will have to get another Master. What are you putting into your heart, mind, and soul? Whatever is coming out is what you are putting in. If we hope for good to come out, we have to put more good in.

7

THE PATTERN EXHIBITED

Jesus is the triumphant example of success in temptation.

We read in Ephesians 6:13, *"Wherefore take unto you the whole armour of God, that ye may be able to withstand in the evil day, and having done all, to stand."* There is great significance to the words, *"evil day"* in this verse. The *"evil day"* is that day in your life when the devil has your destruction on his calendar. There is a day in Jon Jenkins's life and a day in your life, when Satan says, "This is the day that I am going to get him! This is the day that I am going to put a temptation in front of him that he cannot resist." Eve faced such a day, and we are still in trouble today because of her failure.

Matthew 4:1 says, *"Then was Jesus led up of the Spirit into the wilderness to be tempted of the devil."* The *"then"* marks the beginning of Jesus' evil day. Thank God, Jesus did not fail at His evil day. If I understand the Bible correctly, your *"evil day"* may be longer than twenty-four hours – it may be a season. Jesus', *"evil day"* lasted forty days. For forty days, He never took down

His armor. For forty days, He was able to resist the assaults of the evil one. If the perfect Son of God stayed in complete armor for forty days, then it would appear that anything less than that just will not get the job done!

We teach about the whole armor of God, but have you ever really prayed about what the whole armor of God is? The whole armor of God is, in essence, the complete, balanced Christian life in one package – prayer, the helmet of salvation, the sword of the Spirit, the shield of faith, and feet shod with the preparation of the Gospel of peace. The biggest reason that we need to be soul winners is that soul winning is part of a Christian's armor. You will have trouble yielding to temptation if you are a faithful soul winner. A man will not go out and buy a dirty magazine on Thursday morning and then try to win somebody to God on Thursday night. You will always be busy on soul winning night when you are not right with God. It is hard to be vocal in your witness when you know that you have absolutely no help from God.

> *The whole armor of God is, in essence, the complete, balanced Christian life in one package.*

It is no fun to preach when you are not right with God! Behind the pulpit is a pretty dangerous place to stand when you have sin in your life. It is dangerous not only because God might chasten you but also because Satan might get you. He would love to see a loud-mouthed, foolish preacher get up and preach like he has authority when, in reality, he has no protection from the Holy Ghost. I go soul winning as faithfully as I can, not just because

I have a burden for lost people, but also because I have a burden for myself. You may need to reevaluate why you do not go soul winning, why your feet are not shod with the preparation of the Gospel of peace. Are you really a good enough Christian that you can afford the assault of the devil without your armor on? I have a hard enough time keeping the devil off of my back when I *think* I have the armor on. I do not know how long your, *"evil day"* is going to be, but the Lord's *"evil day"* was forty days.

Matthew 4:10 says, *"Then saith Jesus unto him, Get thee hence, Satan: for it is written, Thou shalt worship the Lord thy God, and him only shalt thou serve."* The first word of verse ten is *"then"* Jesus' *"evil day"* had just ended. Maybe your *"evil day"* ends when the devil knows there is no more use in messing with you. Maybe your *"evil day"* ends when the devil has met his match.

Does it seem like you are always falling to the same temptation? Maybe your ***"evil day"*** could end in less than thirty years if you would put up a fight! I beg every child of God losing the battle to temptation to say, "I am going to start being a soul winner. I am going to put on the whole armor of God. I am going to get a prayer life."

Ephesians 6:18 states, *"Praying always with all prayer and supplication in the Spirit. . ."* This confirms that every single piece of armor must be bathed in prayer. Decide that you are going to have on the helmet of salvation, the sword of the Spirit, and that you are going to read and know how to use the Word of God. Three times in chapter four, Jesus said, *"It is written."* He knew what the Scriptures said. Jesus not only **Used The Scriptures** but also

Understood The Scriptures. Notice that the first word in verse eleven is also *"then"*. It says, *"**Then** the devil leaveth him, and, behold, angels came and ministered unto him."* I would rather have angels helping than demons hanging around in my life.

This chapter deals with the fact that our **Saviour Is "Exhibit A"** in **Satan's Effort To Slay**! Our Saviour is the case study. We learned by studying Samson in chapter five how not to battle temptation. We are going to study the Saviour in this chapter and figure out how to defeat temptation. The devil is not playing with us; he is only interested in slaying us! We think that the devil only wants us to fall, but he has a much worse plan than that. The devil wants to kill you! He does not just want to hurt your testimony. He wants to destroy you. The Bible calls him a devourer, someone to be resisted rather than played with.

> *Our Saviour is "Exhibit A" in Satan's effort to Slay!*

Mark 1:13 says of our Saviour, *"And he was there in the wilderness forty days, **tempted of Satan**; and was with the wild beasts; and the angels ministered unto him."* I want to remind you of the words in Hebrews 4:15, *"For we have not an high priest which cannot be touched with the feeling of our infirmities; but was **in all points tempted** like **as we are, yet without sin**."* Satan tempted Him, but He never fell. Our Saviour had forty days of resistance and forty days of victory.

Rather than looking at each of our Saviour's temptations in great detail, we will simply look at them briefly to discern Satan's tactics. I want you to understand Satan's philosophy. In looking at Satan's tactics, I hope you will discover for yourself why God the Holy Spirit led Jesus into the wilderness to be tempted by the devil. God allowed Jesus to be tempted because Jesus is *"Exhibit A"* in this *Eternal Play* – the battle with good and evil.

II Corinthians 2:11 says, *"Lest Satan should get an advantage of us: for we are not ignorant of his devices."* We dare not be ignorant of Satan's devices and tactics. By way of review, let us

The devil is not Playing with us; he is only interested in Slaying us!

consider several things about when and why Jesus was tempted in the wilderness.

1. Jesus Was Tempted After His Obedience.

And it came to pass in those days, that Jesus came from Nazareth of Galilee, and was baptized of John in Jordan. And straightway coming up out of the water, he saw the heavens opened, and the Spirit like a dove descending upon him: And there came a voice from heaven, saying, Thou art my beloved Son, in whom I am well pleased. And immediately the Spirit driveth him into the wilderness.
Mark 1:9-12

Jesus' temptation followed His baptism. Remember that he who most closely *Follows The* Saviour will be most closely *Followed By Satan*! You may have the idea that your

> *What lay before Christ troubled the devil more than what lay behind Christ!*

temptations prove that you are not spiritual. However, you must understand that the more spiritual you become, the greater your temptation will become. It is not the other way around. You will never get separated or spiritual enough to avoid temptation.

Following Jesus' obedience came a *Holy Anointing* and a *Heavenly Approval*. It is only to be expected that the *Anointing* would be followed by an *Assault*. A thief does not rob the poor. The highway robber watches for the man who has plenty. He wants to rob us of our riches, not our rags. The reason that Satan attacked Jesus immediately following His obedience is because he knew the potential of the One with Whom he was dealing.

2. Jesus Was Tempted Before His Opportunity.

> *And he was there in the wilderness forty days, tempted of Satan; and was with the wild beasts; and the angels ministered unto him. Now after that John was put in prison, Jesus came into Galilee, preaching the gospel of the kingdom of God.* **Mark 1:13-14**

Seasons of *Fierce Temptations* are frequently followed by seasons of *Great Triumph*. What *Lay Before* Christ troubled the devil more than what *Lay Behind* Christ. The devil wanted, by any means, to disqualify the One Who was so capable of doing his kingdom the most harm. By defeating the devil, Jesus proved His own worthiness. By conquering the devil, Jesus proved His own competence. He **is** the Lord of glory!

A bridge is proved by weight. A bridge is not built to be a museum piece; it is built to get a load from one side of a body of water to the other side. The way to test a bridge is to put it under the testing or temptation of weight. God allowed Satan to tempt our Saviour to prove to the world Who His Son was. God allows you to be tempted because He thinks you have potential for victory. You may feel defeated because you are being tempted when you should shout because the devil thinks you are a big enough target to mess with. Think that through. We prove gold by putting it in the fire. Likewise, a servant of God is proved by going through temptation.

> *Satan was trying to break down the Saviour's faith in His Father!*

I want you to simply see the pattern that Satan exhibited in ***Going After The Saviour*** and the pattern that the Saviour exhibited in ***Going Against Satan***! It is important to understand the unity of the temptations. These temptations were not completely different – they were three branches of the same tree. Satan tried one technique, and when that did not work, he tried the next one. When that tactic did not work, he tried the last one. These three techniques were completely related to one another.

The reason these temptations were unified and concentrated is because Satan was trying to break down the Saviour's faith in His Father! The reason that Satan wanted to breakdown the

Saviour's faith is found in Hebrews 11:6, *"But without faith it is impossible to please him: for he that cometh to God must believe that he is, and that he is a rewarder of them that diligently seek him."* This was the same tactic used on Job in Job 1:9, *"Then Satan answered the LORD, and said, Doth Job fear God for nought?"* Satan did not have confidence in Job. He said, "God, the only reason that Job loves You and trusts You is because You have been good to him. If You allow me to strip his prosperity, his family, and his health away, we will see how much faith he really has in You."

God said, "Okay, let's try it, but don't touch his body."

Satan took Job's children, his wealth, and everything else he had physically and financially; and Job ended the day on his face worshiping God.

Then Satan came again to God and said, "Well, I guess Job has a little more integrity than I thought, but if you take away his physical health and strength, I know he will not trust You anymore."

God said, "Okay, let's try it, but don't take his life."

Satan took away Job's physical strength. Have you ever thought about the typology between Job and Jesus? I never saw it prior to studying about temptation. Jesus faced a loss of all of his riches for our salvation. *"For ye know the grace of our Lord Jesus Christ, that, though he was rich, yet for your sakes he became poor, that ye through his poverty might be rich."* (II Corinthians 8:9). Did Satan touch our Saviour's body? Did he ever!

Do you understand that Satan is powerful, but he is not all-powerful? He is a great foe, but he is not an omnipotent foe. He reads the Bible and even quotes the Bible, but he does not know the application of the Bible. He would have to know God to know the Bible. Satan does not have any discernment, or he would never have rebelled against God in the first place.

I wonder if Satan thought that Job was Jesus. Thank God for a man who was not Jesus but did not drop the torch! I wonder if the devil has ever thought that you were Jesus. Or, is someone more likely to mistake you for one of the seven sons of Sceva? When they confronted the devil, the Bible says in Acts 19:15, *"And the evil spirit answered and said, Jesus I know, and Paul I know; but who are ye."*

At the end of Job's second temptation battle, he had not only lost physically, but he was also going to lose emotionally. Job 2:9 states, *"Then said his wife unto him, Dost thou still retain thine integrity? curse God, and die."* What an encouragement! Isn't it a blessing when your wife recommends suicide? Allow me to plead with ladies not to give their husbands that kind of advice. I like what Job said in verse 10, *"Thou speakest as one of the foolish women speaketh."* He did not say it in the text, but I think that somewhere between the lines he said, "Shut up, woman! I do not need help being discouraged; I am already discouraged enough."

Then, for thirty chapters, Job's three friends told him that he deserved every thing that had happened to him. They went so far as to say that he deserved worse than he received. Isn't it a blessing when you have friends like that? At one point in Job 16:2 he says, *"I have heard many such things: miserable comforters are ye all."* The Devil was after Jesus' faith just like he was after

page • 201

Job's faith. Remember Job 13:15, *"Though he slay me, yet will I trust in him. . ."* Job said, "I still believe. Old Devil, I still believe! You have not gotten my faith!"

SATAN TRIED TO BREAK DOWN THE SIMPLICITY OF THE SAVIOUR'S FAITH

Then was Jesus led up of the Spirit into the wilderness to be tempted of the devil. And when he had fasted forty days and forty nights, he was afterward an hungred. And when the tempter came to him, he said, If thou be the Son of God, command that these stones be made bread. But he answered and said, It is written, Man shall not live by bread alone, but by every word that proceedeth out of the mouth of God. **Matthew 4:1-4**

Remember what Paul said in II Corinthians 11:3, *"But I fear, lest by any means, as the serpent beguiled Eve through his subtilty, so your minds should be corrupted from the* **simplicity** *that is in Christ."* Paul's great fear for the Corinthian church was that the Devil would manipulate and complicate them so that they no longer had the simple trust and faith to obey God every day. His fear was that Satan would complicate them. I have often said, "Satan moves men and women away from simplicity and toward complexity." Satan does not want us to pray for our daily bread. Satan does not want us to trust God by hour and by day. Satan wants us to be so complicated that we are not even sure of God's existence. The Bible says that in order to be saved we have to become like little children because children are simple.

Many Christian people sometimes do not put much stock in the salvation decisions of children. We get impressed with the adult decisions. The salvations that we should be the least impressed with are adult salvations. You have never seen a child have a jailhouse repentance. Most children are not in jail at four or five years of age. A child's faith is faith in its purest form. If you tell a child what God said, it will be in his heart and in his soul. Jesus said, *"Suffer the little children to come unto me, and forbid them not: for of such is the kingdom of God"* (Matthew 10:14). If we will stay out of a child's way, he will naturally come to God and be saved.

> **Satan moves men and women away from Simplicity and toward Complexity.**

I love the godly men in my church, but if I am ever in a life-or-death situation, I will not call the men of the church to pray for me. If I am in a life-or-death situation, I will call the Beginner Department to ask the boys and girls to pray for me. I know that they can get a prayer through. When you ask a three or four year old child to pray, he does not wonder whether or not he can get a prayer through to heaven. A child just kneels and begins praying like he thinks God is there!

When my children were young, I would pray with each of them each night before they went to bed. As I look back on those years, I almost wish they were small again so I could hear their big prayers. Every one of my children would pray, "Lord, don't let our house burn down tonight." I am not sure why they prayed that, but they did. I remember thinking that they were a bunch of chickens, but as I would walk away, I would think, "Those little children have their whole lives in Your hands, God. They think that if they wake up in the morning it will be because God looked after them during the night." On the other hand, we adults think that we have everything under control.

Satan Tempted Jesus With Selfishness. Satan tried to break down the simplicity of the Saviour's faith by tempting Him to be selfish. Is it not interesting that He who is the *"Bread Of Life"* began His public ministry *Hungry*? Is it not interesting that He Who is called the *"Water Of Life"* ended His earthly ministry *Thirsty*? Everything that Jesus had given to this world, He lived without. Jesus gave us the grace of God that we might build strong families, and He did not have a family. Many of us, because of God's blessings and our obedience to His principles in our life, have beautiful homes, but Jesus did not have a home. Nearly everything that we have because of Jesus, He gave up because of us.

Several summers ago, the Grace Baptist College men's summer tour group and I were at a Bible Camp in Colorado. A river went through the camp in a canyon. At one spot overlooking the canyon, there was a drop, and the river made a turn. The river could not be seen above the drop, and it looked like the water was coming out of a rock with nothing above it. To me, that was a perfect picture of the Lord Jesus Christ. Jesus was the rock that Moses smote twice in the wilderness. I Corinthians 10:4 says, *"And did all drink the same spiritual drink: for they drank of that spiritual Rock that followed them: and that Rock was Christ."* Jesus is the water from which we all drink when we are saved, yet on the cross, Jesus had to say, *"I thirst"* (John 19:28). What an injustice man brought upon the Lord Jesus Christ. The Devil knew what was in front of the Saviour. Gregory of Nazianzus wrote these beautiful words:

He was hungry as a man, yet He fed the hungry as God. He was weary as a man, yet He is our rest as God. He was called a devil as a man,

> *Nearly everything that we have because of Jesus, He gave up because of us.*

yet He cast out devils as God. He prays as man, yet He hears the prayers of man as God. He weeps as a man, yet He dries the tears of man as God. He was sold for thirty pieces of silver as man, yet He redeemed the world as God.

Satan Tempted Jesus With Appetite. It was not a sin for Jesus to be hungry, but to gratify that hunger outside of the will of God would have been a sin! Hebrews 13:4 says, *"Marriage is honourable in all, and the bed undefiled: but whoremongers and adulterers God will judge."* It is not sinful for a husband and wife to smooch. However, it would be sinful for a married person to kiss someone other than his spouse. It was not sinful for Jesus to be hungry. It was not even sinful for Him to want to satisfy that hunger. It was just sinful for Him to fulfill that hunger outside of the boundaries God had set. Satan said, "You haven't eaten for forty days, have You? Look at all those stones there. If thou be the Son of God, command these stones to be made bread and have a feast." Jesus could have done that.

In appealing to Jesus' appetites, Satan was attempting to get the Savior to doubt the providential care of God and deny His dependence upon God. Satan said, "Take it for yourself, Jesus." I wonder how many times God has allowed us to get in a tight spot, perhaps financially, emotionally, or morally. The Devil then came along and said, "You're a child of God. You're saved forever. You're not going to lose your salvation if you take it. Go ahead! You're hungry. Have it." To make the matter even more sinister, the Devil started it all by saying, "By making the stones into bread, you will prove that You are the Son of God."

> *In appealing to Jesus' appetites, Satan was attempting to get the Saviour to doubt the providential care of God and deny His dependence upon God.*

Several years ago, I heard the filthiest thing I have ever heard in my life. A preacher was caught being immoral and is no longer in the ministry. When the churchwoman that he was being immoral with had fears and doubts about what was going on, he said, "You are ministering to the man of God." That is the kind of temptation Jesus was presented with. The devil said, "You're God and you're hungry, so take whatever you want. It's your right. After all, you have given a lot. What's wrong with your taking a little money out of the offering plate? You've worked for your crazy boss, and he hasn't paid you what you're worth, so what is wrong with your lying and stealing some tools? It would really be yours if you were paid what you were worth."

I had one old boy tell me that the reason that he did not tithe was because his wife worked for the Christian school, and she did not get paid what she was worth. So he just figured in his mind what she was worth, and that amount was more than their tithe would have been. So he said that her working in the Christian school was their tithe. This was the same kind of temptation that Jesus had. There are some churches that pay the pastor one amount of money but say that they are going to pay him a higher amount so that he does not have to tithe.

It was not wrong for Jesus to satisfy his hunger, but it was wrong for Him to use the power given to Him for other means to do so! Satan tempted Jesus to do the right thing the wrong way! Bob Jones, Sr. said, "It is never right to do wrong in order to get a chance to do right." The end does not justify the means. Jesus' power was for **Sinner's Redemption**, not for **Selfish Preservation**!

This temptation was paramount to God giving a man a great ability to communicate and lead, but that man builds a business with his ability instead of building a Sunday school class with it. This temptation is tantamount to God giving a man a great ability to communicate, but instead of being a great soul winner with his ability, he becomes a great salesman. Salesmen should be the best soul winners. If a salesman only sells vacuum cleaners or Amway or automobiles instead of putting the same energy into convincing people to accept Christ, he is yielding to the same temptation with which Satan tempted Jesus.

Satan said, "Jesus, you're hungry. You haven't eaten in forty days. Why don't you take a little bit of the power that God the Father gave you to redeem sinners and use it for yourself? You could make the stones into bread and have yourself a meal." Some people will not witness because they are fearful that witnessing would hurt their business. If you are in business and promote yourself in any way, you are a salesman. If God has prospered your business but you have not led someone to God in six months, you should be concerned. Would you be concerned if you had not made one dollar in six months? It should greatly concern you if you have taken all that God has done for you without doing anything for Him in return. God is not against your using the abilities that He has given you to prosper yourself, but prospering yourself is God's secondary purpose for your abilities, not His primary purpose. Matthew 6:33 proves this point: *"But seek ye first the kingdom of God, and his righteousness; and all these things shall be added unto you."* Given a choice between selling a car and seeing a soul saved, a Christian businessman should choose the latter.

Our ***Holiness*** is more important than our ***Happiness***! Our gifts are not for ***Self*** but for ***Service***. Satan often tempts men to starve the spiritual for the material. He often tempts men to beggar the soul by feeding the body. He tempts men to satisfy the stomach by starving the soul! For this reason, Jesus declared, *"Man shall not* *live by bread alone, but by every word that proceedeth out of the mouth of God"* (Matthew 4:4). Jesus said, "Satan, I am hungry, but I am more spiritually hungry than physically hungry. I am not going to take your bait today!" Far too many men rate bread higher than the Bible because God has been so good to them.

Job valued the Bible higher than bread in Job 23:12, *"Neither have I gone back from the commandment of his lips;* ***I have esteemed the words of his mouth more than my necessary food.*** *"* Maybe the reason we are more interested in bread than in the Bible is because God has not allowed us to suffer enough. God could arrange more suffering, if we would like.

What if you had a rule at your house that stated, "No Bible – no breakfast"? If your son knew "No Bible – no breakfast" was true at your house, he would start reading his Bible! For the next thirty years, the motto of every man should be, "No Bible – no bread!" Would you starve to death if you made that motto your own?

> ***Our*** **Holiness** *is more important than our* **Happiness***!*

Far too many Christians have success but no Spirit. They use the gifts that God has given them to get success for themselves. Many of God's people faced with this temptation have crossed the line. They have nice businesses, homes, and automobiles, but they are spiritually empty.

If God has prospered a man's church, it is easy for him to say what the people want to hear in order to keep the crowd coming. Anyone could keep a crowd coming if he acted like a politician.

He could just figure out what the people want and give it to them. There is a problem, though. When a preacher reads His Bible, God tells him what to say. The preacher is just the mailman. It does not matter if the people do not want to hear it. How many churches have been built by a preacher who wanted the crowds more than the anointing? How many preachers have wanted the fame more than the fire? Far too many Christians are wealthy but hungry. Far too many Christians are full but empty. Haggai 1:6 says, *"Ye have sown much, and bring in little; ye eat, but ye have not enough; ye drink, but ye are not filled with drink; ye clothe you, but there is none warm; and he that earneth wages earneth wages to put it into a bag with holes."*

In the devil's first attack on Jesus, he tried to break down the simplicity of the Saviour's faith. He tried to get Him to be selfish.

SATAN TRIED TO BREAK DOWN THE SANITY OF THE SAVIOUR'S FAITH

Then the devil taketh him up into the holy city, and setteth him on a pinnacle of the temple, And saith unto him, If thou be the Son of God, cast thyself down: for it is written, He shall give his angels charge concerning thee: and in their hands they shall bear thee up, lest at any time thou dash thy foot against a stone. Jesus said unto him, It is written again, Thou shalt not tempt the Lord thy God.
Matthew 4:5-7

Satan tried to get the Saviour to be presumptuous. First, he tried to get Jesus to doubt God. When that did not work, he tried to get the Saviour to prove God in a foolish way. He said, "Jump off of this building and see if you survive the fall. If you do not survive, God will raise you up. He said that He would do that for You." Jesus responded, "We are not supposed to tempt the God of heaven." In the first temptation, **Satan Tried To Appeal To The Saviour's Appetite.** In the second temptation, **Satan Tried To Appeal To The Saviour's Adventurous Spirit.** We all have an adventurous side, which is why we were hurt so much as children. Your friends would dare you to jump off of a rock backwards with your eyes closed, and you would do it!

First, Satan tried to rob Jesus of His faith. When that did not work, he tried to turn His faith into sin. First he tried to get him to act in **Self-Preservation**, and then he tried to get Him to act in **Self-Glorification**. We are all the most vulnerable when we are the strongest. If you are in full-time service, the most dangerous thing you will do is to counsel people. While you are giving advice, the devil says, "We are going to see if this old boy knows what he's talking about." I wish everybody was as involved in the work of God as are preachers, but you had better be careful when a disgruntled person comes by to see you. They explain their issues to you, and you think you are just trying to help them. Remember that the devil was thrilled with the answers you gave. Many times I have seen a good, solid Christian get messed up by listening to a disgruntled person vent about their little issue. Then that solid Christian begins to listen to the preaching suspiciously. He begins to expect perfection. The devil tempts us to think that we know more than the man of God.

There was a lady in the Bible who thought that she knew more than the man of God. Her name was Miriam. Moses was the leader, and he married an Ethiopian woman, a woman not of his race. That was not acceptable in the Bible, and the entire leadership of Moses' government became critical of him because of that marriage. Miriam, Moses' sister, said, "You know, God speaks to us just like He speaks to Moses. Moses is not God; he's just a man." The problem was that Moses was God's man. Although Moses was just a man, if Moses was in trouble, God would take care of him, not Miriam. While Miriam was being presumptuous, God struck her with leprosy. Prior to her criticism of the man of God, Miriam had some influence. As a leper, she had no influence. She could not approach people. She had to live outside of town and call out, "Unclean! Unclean!" Moses had to beg God to take away Miriam's leprosy.

Isn't it interesting that we are often the most vulnerable when we are the strongest? Following are some Biblical examples of men who were strong yet vulnerable:

➢ **Moses.** He was the meekest man on the earth, but in anger, he struck the rock twice and lost his entrance into the Promised Land.

➢ **Elijah.** He was so bold that he stood against an entire nation of false prophets, yet within twenty-four hours he was running for his life because one woman was after him.

➢ **Peter.** He pledged the most intense loyalty to the Savior, yet he was the first one to curse and deny knowing the Lord.

These men are proof that we are the most vulnerable when we are the strongest.

God gives us **Liberty** but not a **License**. God offers **Protection**, but He does not allow **Presumption**. I believe in eternal security, but many Christians have turned eternal security into a license to sin. If you know that something is a sin and do it anyway, that is called presumptuous sin.

To trust God is faith, but to tempt God is presumption. It does not please God that some Christians walk so close to the edge. Are you as separated as you are supposed to be? Or, do you have a different standard by which you live when you are away from your church family? Ladies that dress one way in their hometown and another way out of town are sinning presumptuously. A lady who changes her dress standards according to where she is because she does not want to lose her influence is tempting God.

He who courts temptation invites his own ruin! Draw the line! I plead with businessmen to draw the line. Make your line so obvious that you cannot blow it. I have a policy that I will not counsel alone with a woman. If a lady comes to see me, she has to come during my organized counseling times when either my wife or my secretary is sitting outside of my door, one turn of the doorknob from watching what happens. You cannot be too careful because we are living in a fallen world.

Many men of God have fallen into adultery because of their counseling. As they give everybody counsel they begin to think that they are strong. The devil wants you to think that you are strong. He says, "Tell that broken woman that you love her and understand her hurt. Tell her. Tell her again." Before long, that lady will want more than verbal encouragement, she will want some physical touch as well. If a lady comes to me for counseling, I sit behind my desk. If a woman wants repeated counseling appointments with me, then my wife has to be in the meetings. I want my wife in the meetings for two reasons:

1. *I want to protect my testimony.*
2. *My wife has unusual perception.*

Many women who want repeated counseling do not want help; they want attention. When a preacher does not discern that, he is setting himself up for disaster. If a woman ever says to me, "Preacher, I need to see you and no one else", I get scared. I send them to my wife. She is a sweet, kind lady who sees directly to the heart of the matter. She listens for a while and then says, "Do you read your Bible? How in the world are you expecting to be a good wife if you don't read your Bible? Do you pray?" She tells them to get right with God! If a woman will not see my wife, I do not see them again.

> *He who courts temptation invites his own ruin!*

SATAN TRIED TO BREAK DOWN THE STABILITY OF THE SAVIOUR'S FAITH

Again, the devil taketh him up into an exceeding high mountain, and sheweth him all the kingdoms of the world, and the glory of them; And saith unto him, All these things

will I give thee, if thou wilt fall down and worship me. Then saith Jesus unto him, Get thee hence, Satan: for it is written, Thou shalt worship the Lord thy God, and him only shalt thou serve. Then the devil leaveth him, and, behold, angels came and ministered unto him.
Matthew 4:8-11

First, Satan tried to tempt Jesus to be ***Selfish By Using Appetite***. Second, Satan tried to tempt Jesus to be ***Presumptuous By Using Adventure***. Third, Satan tried to tempt Jesus to ***Compromise By Using Ambition***. Satan tempted the Saviour to lower His standards to increase His influence. Satan knew that one day Jesus would rule and reign on the earth, so he said, "Come up here, Jesus, to this high mountain so that I can show you all the world and its kingdoms. If you will bow down and worship me, you will not have to go to the cross. You won't have to go through all the trouble ahead of you. I'll give it to you right now. You can have it without going to Calvary. You can bypass the cross and have the world right now! Jesus, take the easy way out." That is exactly what he does with us as well.

> ➢ To the **college student** Satan says, "Don't go to college for four years and have to struggle and pray and beat your head against the wall. Just leave college your first semester and go be a preacher! Someone as gifted as you – you are D. L. Moody incarnated anyway."

> ➢ Satan tempts the **church member** to say, "I have been a member of this church for three months, why am I not the deacon chairman?"

> To the **employee** Satan says, "I'll make you head of the company before you have even earned minimum wage."

Satan tempted Jesus to **Endanger His Integrity** to **Enlarge His Influence**. This temptation was to choose the easy conquest. The suffering, the cat of nine tails, His beard being plucked out, His being spit on, His being punched in the face, the crown of thorns could have all been avoided had Jesus yielded to Satan's temptation. Satan tempted Jesus to take the line of least resistance, to **Reach For The Crown** by **Rescinding The Cross.** Satan tempted Him to attain the power without paying the price, to gain success without sacrifice! That is the greatest lie of the devil. There is no free lunch. There is no easy way to the top. Everybody that gets to the top quickly also falls quickly.

> *Satan tempted the Saviour to lower His standards to increase His influence!*

God does not trust most of us with money because we love to spend money, and when God speaks to us about giving, we have no money left to give. As soon as we get a pay raise, we immediately figure out how our standard of living will go up. Instead, we should say, "God, you gave me the extra money so I could do more for You. How do You want me to spend this extra money?" Most of us wish we had a rich relative that would die quickly so that we could be like the millions of others who have gotten wealth quickly and ruined their lives. The wonderful thing about having money when you are older is that you have worked hard to get it and you have the character to handle it.

If God has prospered you financially, give all of your money away before you die so that your children do not ruin their lives fighting over it. If I have any money left at the end of my road, I am going to give it to the work of God. In fact, some Christians make their church the beneficiary of their resources because they do not want to ruin their children.

> *From that time forth began Jesus to shew unto his disciples, how that he must go unto Jerusalem, and suffer many things of the elders and chief priests and scribes, and be killed, and be raised again the third day. Then Peter took him, and began to rebuke him, saying, Be it far from thee, Lord: this shall not be unto thee. But he turned, and said unto Peter, Get thee behind me, Satan: thou art an offence unto me: for thou savourest not the things that be of God, but those that be of men.* **Matthew 16:21-23**

> **Satan tempted Jesus to reach for the Crown by dodging the Cross.**

Jesus called Peter Satan because Peter was talking like Satan. Jesus had to go to Calvary, and when Peter tried to suggest otherwise, Jesus said, "Satan put those words in your mouth!" If there is going to be a resurrection, there has to be a crucifixion. If there is going to be victory, there has to be a battle. If there is going to be a prize, there has to be a fight. If there is going to be a coronation day, there has to be a training time.

Parents, we have to stop rearing children with no character. We want our children to have good lives. Because we love them, we are tempted to give to them. Love gives. John 3:16 says, *"For God so loved the world, that he **gave** his only begotten Son, that whosoever believeth in him should not perish, but have everlasting life."* The great danger is that if we give too much, we will raise people with no character. People with no character fall like flies when they are tempted by the devil. People with no character pursue what they want without contemplating the cost.

Thank God that in Matthew 26:39 Jesus said, *"O my Father, if it be possible, let this cup pass from me: nevertheless not as I will, but as thou wilt."* Jesus said, "Dad, I'll try to drink it. I'll do the best I can." The first temptation was to be selfish. The second temptation was to be presumptuous. The final temptation was to compromise.

The temptation to compromise comes to all of us every day.

- ➢ To the pastor in his study
- ➢ To the laborer at his work
- ➢ To the student in his studies
- ➢ To the employer in his business
- ➢ To the parent in the home
- ➢ To the young person in his testimony

We are all tempted to leave the straight line of duty, service, faithfulness, loyalty, integrity, honor, and truth. Compromise tempts us to be silent when we should speak up for fear of offending. Compromise prompts us to tolerate sin to keep the offerings of the church strong. Compromise prompts us to set men over the offices of the church because of their social positions rather than because of their spiritual qualifications. Then the deacon board turns into a board of directors rather than a group of prayers, soul winners, and servants of God.

Churches that compromise for any of these reasons are worshiping Satan. Do you think that God would bring revival to a church involved in Satan worship? You may not worship the Devil, but if you bow down for the sake of bypassing the cross, you will back up and not say it straight in order to get the crown without the sacrifice.

One of the reasons that we started Grace Baptist College was to train young men to understand that in small towns one has to be honest and ethical. You cannot be success-oriented at the expense of truth. All across the country, there is a proliferation of churches selling out lock, stock, and barrel to keep the crowds coming. These are churches that take the name Baptist off their sign to attract more people. They also replace hymns with watered down choruses. It should be a cold day where the booger man lives before we are singing choruses written by a twenty-one-year-old punk and putting Fanny Crosby out to pasture. It should be a cold day where the booger man lives when we start listening to contemporary music while putting P. P. Bliss and all the great hymn writers out to pasture. It may attract a crowd, but we would be bypassing the cross for the crown. I would rather have a church built on the truth than a church built on toys and trinkets. The only way to build a work of God is to preach the truth of the Word of God.

We have looked at "Exhibit A" in this temptation. Satan went after the **Simplicity Of Christ's Faith**, the **Sanity Of His Faith**, and the **Stability Of His Faith**. Satan is after the same three things in your life. He wants you to compromise. If you will not yield, then he wants you to be proud and use your faith as a shield to do something presumptuously.

8

PREVAILING EMBRACED

Let us embrace the victory that Christ has already won.

These things I have spoken unto you, that in me ye might have peace. In the world ye shall have tribulation: but be of good cheer; I have overcome the world. **John 16:33**

The words *"these things"* in this verse are referring to the Scriptures. Peace is the end result of successful warfare. When Jesus says, *"These things I have spoken unto you, that in me ye might have peace,"* He is referring to the role of the Word of God in our victory over temptation.

Tribulation means "trouble that comes from testing or temptation." We all have trouble, tribulation, and temptation in the Christian life. However, we *can* be victorious in the battle against temptation! Would you like to bury your besetting sin once and for all? You may think that victory will never happen, and it will not happen outside of the promises of God's Word. Jesus gave us the Bible for one reason – to have victory. Following that victory, you can declare peace. In the world, we *will* have trouble, tribulation, and temptation; however, if Jesus said that He has overcome the world, then I am going to believe that we also can overcome.

I want to embrace the victory that Jesus won when He prevailed over temptation. The victory that we need can only be found by our faith, and our faith is based upon the Scripture. This is evident from these verses:

Who gave himself for our sins, that he might deliver us from this present evil world, according to the will of God and our Father. **Galatians 1:4**

Ye are of God, little children, and have overcome them: because greater is he that is in you, than he that is in the world. **I John 4:4**

For whatsoever is born of God overcometh the world: and this is the victory that overcometh the world, even our faith. **I John 5:4**

You have to first believe in the **Possibility Of Victory** to experience the **Possession Of Victory.** I am not a charismatic, but if you do not believe you can win the victory, then you will not win the victory. Men that battle with immoral thoughts and pornography need to envision the day when the battle is won. Whatever you battle with – lust, envy, jealousy, gossip, dishonesty, stealing – believe that you can win the victory. When the Bible says, *"Now faith is the substance of things hoped for, the evidence of things not seen"* (Hebrews 11:1), it is simply saying that I have to believe a thing before I experience it. I have to view myself as being victorious. I have to view myself as a conqueror.

We will never conquer our failures, passions, or our powerful foe with willpower alone. We must have a will to win in order to be victorious, but willpower alone is not enough. The Devil has a stronger will than we do. It is a fact that we need faith, which produces the vision to succeed, but where do we get that faith? *"So then faith cometh by hearing, and hearing by the word of God"* (Romans 10:17). Victory requires Word power not Willpower.

> *Victory requires Word power not Will power.*

How did Jesus prevail? Can we embrace that same victory for ourselves? I believe the answer is a resounding "Yes!" The secret is in His victorious confrontation over Satan's temptation. Three times Jesus responded to the devil's temptations with the words *"It is written."* In Matthew 4:4, Matthew 4:7, and Matthew 4:10, Jesus declared His faith was in the Word of God. Let us look at each of these occurrences and embrace the same victory that Jesus Himself experienced.

His Preparation - He Was Filled With The Scriptures

But he answered and said, It is written, Man shall not live by bread alone, but by every word that proceedeth out of the mouth of God. **Matthew 4:4**

You cannot whip the devil if you do not have enough Bible inside. Imagine those long, silent years of Jesus' life in Nazareth. We know almost nothing of His childhood or teen years. God did not tell us about those years in the life of Jesus because the preparation is always private.

Speaking of musical ability, Dr. Jack Hyles used to say, "Greatness is not in the performance but in the preparation." The people who defeat temptation are not the ones with the talent, but rather the ones who, in silence, quiet, and private, win the victory in their thought life. Jesus, no doubt, daily and diligently studied the Old Testament writings, storing away in His mind their precious truths. No wonder He was able to reach into His quiver and pull out sharp arrows to shoot at the enemy.

Jesus whipped the Devil because He knew the Bible better than the Devil. Do you know the Bible better than the Devil? While he knows the Book, human psychology, and our weaknesses, the one thing the Devil does not have is wisdom. Wisdom is the ability to apply the truths of the Word of God to life. The Devil may know the Bible, but he does not have enough wisdom to know how to use it properly. A child of God bathed in the Word of God that has dived deep into the Scriptures and filled his mind with the Word of God can withstand the temptations of the Devil.

The one great passage of Scripture about Jesus' childhood is found in Luke 2:42-47.

And when he was twelve years old, they went up to Jerusalem after the custom of the feast. And when they had fulfilled the days, as they returned, the child Jesus tarried behind in Jerusalem; and Joseph and his mother knew not of it. But they, supposing him to have been in the company, went a day's journey; and they sought him among their kinsfolk and acquaintance. And when they found him not, they turned back again to Jerusalem, seeking him. And it came to pass, that after three days they found him in the temple, sitting in the midst of the doctors, both hearing them, and asking them questions. And all that heard him were astonished at his understanding and answers.

By the age of twelve, Jesus could out-do, out-wit, and out-reason the great Scribes, Pharisees, and Old Testament teachers of the nation of Israel. The great learned men of the law were no match for Him. Where did He get that preparation?

I cannot help but remember all that took place at Jesus' birth. The Bible says in Luke 2:19, *"But Mary kept all these things, and pondered them in her heart."* I have no doubt that when the wise men headed home, Mary looked at Joseph and said, "We have our hands full. We have to put enough Bible in this boy so that He can pass the testing. I do not know what is ahead of Him, but I think He is going to face some dark and difficult days."

Parents, we are all preparing our children for success, and that is why most of them will fail. Mary did not train Jesus for success; she trained Jesus for failure. She prepared him for dark days, not high days. We have to teach our children to respond properly in disappointment. I do not like to lose any more than anybody else. I like to win at everything I try. However, if you only know how to win, you will be a lousy person. You have to learn how to rebound from failure. If you do not know what to put into your children, start with the B-I-B-L-E. We teach our children the song; now teach them the Book about which the song is written.

> *Mary did not train Jesus for success; she trained Jesus for failure.*

If you are a father, perhaps you need to repent of your failure to teach your children the Bible. Deuteronomy 6:7 says,

And thou shalt teach them diligently unto thy children, and shalt talk of them when thou sittest in thine house, and when thou walkest by the way, and when thou liest down, and when thou risest up.

The Word of God is to be the primary source of conversation in your family! We are all prone to get busy and forget our number one job. That job is not to make money or to build houses, it is to take the Bible and plant it so deep in our children's hearts that they will be able to handle the dark days. Every parent will see his children go through adversity.

Dr. Tom Vogel of Hyles-Anderson College in Crown Point, Indiana has a son who was visiting on a bus route in Chicago for the First Baptist Church of Hammond. While he and a few other young men were driving back to the Hammond area through a gangland neighborhood, a bullet went into the car and through Brother Vogel's son's temples. Though critically injured at the time, the wound healed, leaving little permanent damage. Today that boy is serving God in the ministry.

If the average Christian young person were shot in the head, they would say, "Why did God do that to me? I was serving God! Why didn't He do a better job of taking care of me?" That is not what this young man did. He came out of that experience shouting the victory!

Something will happen in your child's future that will be a dark experience. Someone will die or get hurt; there will be reversal or bad news from a doctor. Our children have free wills that we cannot control; however, we can control how much Bible they get. Fathers, repent to your family if you have allowed family devotions to slip, and set out afresh and anew to teach your children the Word of God every single day.

Why not start a contest with your young men to see how much Scripture they can memorize? Fanny Crosby memorized five chapters a week, and she had a disadvantage because she was blind. Many of us have not memorized five verses in six months, and we wonder why we fall and fail and struggle. If Jesus needed the Scripture, so do we. Jesus is the One that said, *"Man shall not live by bread alone, but by every word that proceedeth out of the mouth of God."*

A Jewish boy became a man at age thirteen. That is not true in America. It took ten men to constitute a synagogue. Once a Jewish boy reached the age of thirteen, he was legally and ecclesiastically able to stand as one of the ten men in a synagogue. When a man starts a church today, if he has five adults and five teenagers, he does not say that he has ten men. Rather, he says, "I have five men and five boys." Young men need to decide that no matter what their parents have or have not taught them, they will get enough Scripture in their hearts and souls to make something of their lives! I know what young men deal with – the flesh, the Internet, and all the filth. This is one of the hardest periods in history to have a pure mind. Some parents would be shocked if they knew what their boys know. Many sons act innocent out of respect for their parents, but their mind is after the flesh.

A preacher who raised his family with great convictions and put a lot of Bible into his children said to me, "While my kids were growing up, I was not afraid to see if what I was putting in was enough." Most parents are so insecure that they will not let their child test what they are putting into them. They protect their children so severely that they will only have one shot. At that point, if they have failed, it will be too late to change anything. He told me, "I sat my daughter down when she was thirteen years of age and asked her if she believed what I believed." She was polite, but hesitant, she responded with a "yes". The preacher said, "If this is true, convince me from the Scriptures why you believe the same thing that I do." At that point, he listed eight or nine different convictions. She agreed with him on every issue but one. She said, "Dad, I do not know that I have a conviction that it is wrong for me as a woman to wear pants." She was expecting a bomb to go off, but her wise father chuckled at her and said, "Amen, now I know what I need to work on!"

About three years later he sat her down again and had the same conversation. She was still not convinced that she should not wear pants once she was out on her own. He said, "That's okay, sweetheart. I think you are wrong, and I think I can prove that you are wrong. But I don't have a problem with that." He did not agree with her, but he realized that he was engaged in spiritual warfare. He had to win the battle with prayer and the Scriptures, not with pressure and intimidation.

> *He had to win the battle with prayer and the Scriptures, not with pressure and intimidation.*

He filled her life with as much Bible as he could about those issues, but he never brought it up again. When they walked forward at the wedding altar, as he was ready to give her away, she said, "Dad, before you kiss me, and give me away, I want to tell you something. It's my conviction now. No pants for me."

Parents cannot cram their convictions down the throats of their children. They can only trust the Word of God. If we put the Bible into our children, it will not return void. We tell our children that they have to believe one thing, then another, and then still another. Why don't we just put enough Bible into our children that the Spirit of God tells them what to believe? The reason they walk out of our homes and say, "Well, that was just never my conviction" is because we did not put enough Bible into them.

Jewish boys were taught the law by their fathers beginning at age three. They were also taught a trade. In the book of Mark, Jesus was called *"the carpenter"*. He was a tradesman. When Jesus went to Calvary, He was a man. At thirty years of age, He could hold down a job that he had learned at the hand of his daddy. Men need to teach their boys something – how to change a tire, how to change oil, how to wire a house. They need to teach their boys something that will give them value. If your boy wants to go to a gym to work out, you should evaluate whether or not that is a good idea. Not all of the women lifting weights at the gym think about modesty. If a boy wants to work out, let him get a job working for a contractor who needs stacks of OSB taken up to the roof of a house.

In Jesus' day, by the age of six, He would have gone to a synagogue where he would have sat in a semicircle on the floor listening to the rabbis repetitiously read and explain the law and the Old Testament Talmud. From the age of six on, Jesus would have sat for five or six hours a day hearing the Bible. I am not against the things we do to make the Bible more appealing, but it is a shame that we have to entertain people to keep them interested. Jesus would have attended such a synagogue until age fifteen. *"And he came to Nazareth, where he had been brought up: and, as his custom was, he went into the synagogue on the sabbath day, and stood up for to read"* (Luke 4:16).

Jesus went into the synagogue because that was His *"custom"* or habit. Upon entering the synagogue, Jesus stood up and read

page • 230

the Scriptures. He was able to do that not because He was the God-man, but because it was part of His preparation. Jesus was raised in the Bible.   His entire childhood was immersed in the Scriptures. Can you imagine an eight or nine year old boy saying, "Let's sit down and talk about soteriology. I am intrigued about that doctrine of predestination and how it ties in with election and the free will of man. What about that perseverance of the saints? What about Calvinism?" Seven and eight year old boys are not interested in Bible doctrines because seventy and eighty year old fathers and grandfathers are not interested in them either. They could, regrettably, tell you the scoring average of every player on their favorite sports team.

Young preachers very rarely impress us with their understanding of Bible doctrine. They sure can mimic exciting preachers, though. Why are we so bankrupt when it comes to the Scriptures? In no other way and with no other weapon can we be prepared for the conflict! The devil does not announce his onslaughts in advance. He does not give us time for Bible study. He shows up when we least expect it, at our weakest moment. Our only hope is to be fully equipped with the Sword of the Spirit in our hand and with enough wisdom and understanding to use it properly. In repelling the assaults of the Devil, our Lord did not appeal to **Inward Illumination** but to **Written Revelation**!

When David killed Goliath, he went with five smooth stones from the brook. He only used one to kill his adversary. Jesus had five books of the Bible, the Pentateuch, with which to defeat His adversary the Devil. All three of His responses were direct quotes from the book of Deuteronomy. He only needed one book!

David had four to spare, and Jesus had four to spare!

It is important to highlight Satan's tactic. In Matthew 4:6, Satan quoted Scripture:

> *And saith unto him, If thou be the Son of God, cast thyself down: for it is written, He shall give his angels charge concerning thee: and in their hands they shall bear thee up, lest at any time thou dash thy foot against a stone.*

Jesus countered the Devil's temptation with Scripture. The Devil's heart is full of rebellion! He always acts out of self-interest.

The diabolical ingenuity that the Devil used in quoting Psalm 91 is amazing. He misquoted and misapplied the passage of Scripture that actually says, *"For he shall give his angels charge over thee, to keep thee in all thy ways"* (Psalm 91:11). The devil cunningly omitted the last part of the verse. In doing so, he changed the whole complexion of the passage to make it look as if his advice were the will of God. The Devil tried to make it look as if Psalm 91:11 was an unconditional promise. The reality is that the promise is conditional. He perverted the Scriptures.

Do not use the Bible to justify your self-willed decisions. So many think God is leading them because they have "peace" about it. Where in the Bible does peace ever precede the will of God? Paul said in I Corinthians 16:9, *"For a great door and effectual is opened unto me, and there are many adversaries."* You know you are in the will of God if you are facing opposition. If everything is easy, the Devil is making it so that you slip right out of the will of God. Calvary was the will of God, but it was not an easy or pleasant journey. There were probably many times that Jesus said, "Dad, I don't have peace about this." The devil does not want you to know that he is often the one speaking to you. He will even quote enough Bible for you to think that what he is saying is spiritual, and then he will lead you right off a cliff.

In China's later Han era, there lived a politician by the name of Yang Zhen, a man known for his upright character. After he was made a provincial governor, one of his earlier patrons, Wang Mi, paid him an unexpected visit. As they talked over old times, Wang Mi brought out a beautiful golden cup and presented it to Yang Zhen. Yang Zhen refused to accept it because he felt that there would be strings attached to the gift. Wang Mi persisted, saying, "There's no one here tonight but you and me, so no one will know."

"You say that no one will know," Yang Zhen replied, "but that is not true. Heaven will know, and you and I will know, too." Wang Mi was ashamed, and backed down. Subsequently, Yang Zhen's integrity won increasing recognition, and he rose to a high post in the central government.

Human nature is weak, and we tend to yield to temptation when we think no one else will see or know. In fact, if there were no police force, many people would not hesitate to steal. Leaders need courage born of integrity in order to be capable of powerful and effective spiritual leadership. To achieve this courage, you need to read your Bible and pray every day, just as the children's song states. You need to fall in love with your Bible.

His Inspiration - He Was Filled With The Spirit

Jesus said unto him, It is written again, Thou shalt not tempt the Lord thy God. **Matthew 4:7**

This word *tempt* means "to put on trial, to injure, or to inflict with an insult". Jesus said, "I dare not insult God! I dare not put my Father on trial! I dare not inflict injury on one so important to my survival." Jesus was not only **Filled With The Scriptures**, but he was also **Filled With The Spirit**. Hebrews 1:9 says, *"Thou hast loved righteousness, and hated iniquity; therefore God, even thy God, hath anointed thee with the oil of gladness above thy fellows."* Jesus was filled with more power and anointing than any other man that had ever lived. That filling and anointing was not because He was the God-man but rather because He loved righteousness and hated iniquity more than anybody else did. The sweet Spirit of God is not Someone that we can insult or injure without great consequences!

II Timothy 3:16 states, *"All scripture is given by inspiration of God, and is profitable for doctrine, for reproof, for correction, for instruction in righteousness."* The word *inspiration* means "God-breathed" or "the breath of God." We believe in the divine inspiration of the Bible, meaning that God literally breathed every word of the Bible into the ears of holy men of old. The Holy Spirit of God is a worker. Acts 2:2 says, *"And suddenly there came a sound from heaven as of a rushing mighty wind, and it filled all the house where they were sitting."* We cannot take for granted the breath of God!

Matthew 3:16 says, *"And Jesus, when he was baptized, went up straightway out of the water: and, lo, the heavens were opened unto him, and he saw the Spirit of God descending like a dove, and lighting upon him."* The Holy Spirit here is pictured like a dove. The dove is the only bird without a gallbladder. The purpose of the gallbladder is to store bile, a bitter substance produced by our bodies. Our flesh is a producer of bitterness. The dove has no capacity to store bitterness. The gallbladder keeps bitterness from killing the body. God so designed His Spirit so as not to have the capacity to store bitterness.

You cannot grieve, quench, resist, or ignore the Holy Spirit of God without losing His power. He is too tender and sensitive of a Person. Jesus won the battle over temptation because He was full of power! Jesus was not weak and half empty. He was overflowing! Jesus walked into the forty days of temptation with the power of the Spirit of God upon His life! As a Spirit-filled man Jesus **Entered The Temptation**, and as a Spirit-filled man Jesus **Escaped It Triumphant**. If Jesus Christ needed Spirit-filling to battle the Devil, how do we expect to defeat the Devil without Spirit-filling?

A gentleman had a pet dove, which would light upon his shoulder, walk down his arm, and eat out of his hand. One day, he decided to experiment with his dove. As it was eating out of his hand, he gripped it a little too tightly. When he relaxed his grip, the dove flew away and lighted upon a tree. It looked sad. The man coaxed and called. After much pleading, the dove very reluctantly came back. Once again, the man was rough with the dove. The dove again flew away and acted as before, but this time the man had to call and coax much longer. It seemed the dove would never return, but it finally did. Again the man repeated his roughness with the dove. When he relaxed his grip, the dove again flew farther away and lighted upon a tree. It drooped its wings and looked perplexed and grieved. The man began to coax and call, but the dove lifted its wings and flew away, never to return.

> As a Spirit-filled man Jesus **Entered the Temptation,** *and as a* Spirit-filled man Jesus **Escaped it Triumphant.**

The Lord said in Genesis 6:3, *"My spirit shall not always strive with man."* The Holy Spirit is a comforter and helper. He does not fight with people but rather helps them. If you quench Him and resist Him and rough Him up with bitterness and anger, you will run Him right out of your world. You will lose your will to do right because you will have lost your power. Saul ran the Holy Spirit out of his life and never got Him back. Saul was Israel's king for two years when he ran the Holy Ghost off with his disobedience. He then reigned as Israel's king for thirty-eight additional years without the Holy Spirit's influence. He was simply a puppet who hurt everybody around him, including the next king. He was an old, bitter, mean, grouchy, formerly Spirit-filled monarch.

Ephesians 5:18 says, *"And be not drunk with wine, wherein is excess; but be filled with the Spirit."* Are you filled with the Holy Spirit? God parallels fullness of the Holy Spirit with drunkenness.

If you were drunk with wine, there would be evidence ***Externally*** that you were under the influence of alcohol ***Internally***. Is there any evidence in your life that you are under the Holy Spirit's influence? When somebody is under the influence, they are loud and they are not afraid of anything. Holy Spirit fullness will cause you to go soul winning and knock on somebody's door like you are not afraid of anything. Holy Spirit fullness will give you courage where you once had fear.

As a Spirit-filled man, Jesus entered the temptation; and, as a Spirit-filled man, He escaped triumphantly. Jesus ordered the enemy off the field in Matthew 4:10-11, *"Then saith Jesus unto him, Get thee hence, Satan: for it is written, Thou shalt worship the Lord thy God, and him only shalt thou serve. Then the devil leaveth him, and, behold, angels came and ministered unto him."* The Devil retreated - exhausted and defeated! The Devil is the one that should be exhausted and defeated, not us! Jesus proved that we can not win a ***Crown Without A Conflict Waged***, and He proved that there is no ***Triumph Without A Temptation Won***!

HIS DETERMINATION - HE WAS FILLED WITH A SERVANT'S HEART

Then saith Jesus unto him, Get thee hence, Satan: for it is written, Thou shalt worship the Lord thy God, and him only shalt thou serve. **Matthew 4:10**

Jesus was not only filled with the Scriptures and the Spirit, but He was also filled with a servant's heart. The last words of Jesus' temptation were, *"and him only shalt thou serve."* Philippians 2:7 says of our Savior, *"But made himself of no reputation, and took upon him the form of a servant, and was made in the likeness of men."*

> *You will never defeat temptation by resistance alone.*

Someone has rightly said, "An idle mind is the Devil's workshop!" You will never defeat temptation by resistance alone. Defeating temptation also requires replacement! If Friday nights are tough on you because you used to go to the bar, get involved in a program or ministry on Friday night. Get rid of the bottle by replacing it with something spiritual. Get involved in serving God!

> *And he that sent me is with me: the Father hath not left me alone; for I do always those things that please him.* **John 8:29**

> *I must work the works of him that sent me, while it is day: the night cometh, when no man can work.* **John 9:4**

> *Jesus saith unto them, My meat is to do the will of him that sent me, and to finish his work.* **John 4:34**

> *I have glorified thee on the earth: I have finished the work which thou gavest me to do.* **John 17:4**

Jesus was a worker! I love some of the chronological capsules we see about His life. In one place, He was busy all day long healing people. Matthew 12:15 says, *"But when Jesus knew it, he withdrew himself from thence: and great multitudes followed him, and he healed them all."* Jesus had been running a thousand miles an hour for thirty-six hours straight. Then He said to His disciples,

> *Come ye yourselves apart into a desert place, and rest a while: for there were many coming and going, and they had no leisure so much as to eat. And he said unto them, Come ye yourselves apart into a desert place, and rest a while: for there were many coming and going, and they had no leisure so much as to eat. And they departed into a desert place by ship privately. And the people saw them departing, and many knew him, and ran afoot thither out of all cities, and outwent them, and came together unto him. And Jesus, when he came out, saw much people, and was moved with compassion toward them, because they were as sheep not having a shepherd: and he began to teach them many things.* **Mark 6:31-34**

Although Jesus was seeking rest, He preached to the people. Then, when He had finished preaching, He fed 5,000 men, besides women and children. Jesus had been up nearly forty-eight hours at this time. He put His disciples on a boat, *"And when he had sent them away, he departed into a mountain to pray"* (Mark 6:46). Jesus was a worker!

One day He had been running so hard for so many days that His mother and brethren came to get Him because they feared He would die because He was not taking care of Himself. Upon discovering that His mother and brethren wanted to see Him, Jesus said, *"For whosoever shall do the will of my Father which is in heaven, the same is my brother, and sister, and mother"* (Matthew 12:50). Jesus did not even want to recognize His family if they were going to stop Him from working! Jesus was a worker. No wonder He was a successful warrior as well.

We think that if we work hard we will not have any energy when, in reality, the opposite is true. Isaiah 40:31 states, *"But they that wait upon the LORD shall renew their strength; they shall mount up with wings as eagles; they shall run, and not be weary; and they shall walk, and not faint."* To wait upon the Lord is to serve the Lord, just as a waitress serves the customer in the restaurant. Waiting on the Lord is doing what He told you to do and waiting for the next orders.

You will never defeat Satan successfully until you determine to serve the Savior. God does not give **His Power To Impress**; He gives **His Power To Express**. Paul said in Romans 1:16, *"For I am not ashamed of the gospel of Christ: for it is the power of God unto salvation to every one that believeth; to the Jew first, and also to the Greek."* The message contains the power, not the messenger. God will only give you His power if you are going to need it. If you are going to store His power in a pond, He will not give it to you. God's power is not to be reserved. His power is to flow through us. You only get God's power when you serve Him.

"But ye have an unction from the Holy One, and ye know all things" (I John 2:20). Holy Spirit fullness is called unction. You will not have **Unction** if you do not also have **Function**! God gives us the unction so that we can be His servants successfully. Are you a servant of God? What did you do for God this week? If you get paid for your service, then you are not a true servant. True service for God is performed on Sunday mornings, Sunday nights, mid-week Bible study night, and soul winning night. True service for God is rendered on a volunteer basis! Are you a servant of God? Whose life have you changed? Who is going to Heaven because of your service? You cannot lick the Devil because you are not a servant.

The busier I get for God, the less time I have to sin. When I am on the computer writing a sermon, I do not check out a dirty Internet site to get some inspiration for my sermon! You will probably not stop to get a pack of cigarettes on the way to go soul winning.

> *God does not give His power to Impress; He gives His power to Express.*

A young man had been battling pornography. He went to a drugstore to look at the dirty magazines on the rack. He knew that it was wrong, but he had been struggling. The next week, he went out soul winning with his church. When he knocked on the door of the first house, the druggist from the drugstore opened the door! If that young man had known he would knock on the druggist's door, he probably would not have gone soul winning that night. However, if he had known he would knock on the druggist's door, maybe he would have never stopped by the drugstore at all.

You will not yield to temptation and serve God simultaneously. Serving God is an important ingredient to your success as a Christian. Do not wait until you have victory in all areas before you begin to serve God. Serving God can be a motivation to someone to stop doing wrong. Are you a servant of God?

A. B. Earle told an interesting story. One night during a terrible storm at sea that threatened at every moment to sink the ship, one of the ship's crew members was trying to close a hatch on deck. While trying to save the ship from sinking, a wave struck the man with great force, carrying him into the raging sea. Although he was a good swimmer, he was so disabled that he could only keep above water. They saw him lifting up his hands through the white foam, signifying his desire for help, but the captain said, "Don't lower a boat, for no small boat can live in this sea in this terrific storm. We cannot save the man. The most we can do is to save the ship."

The vessel was bearing farther and farther from the helpless man. Once more, the crew members saw his imploring hands come up among the white caps further off, which moved all hearts that witnessed it. Still the Captain said that a small boat must not be lowered, as it could not survive a moment in the treacherous storm. One of the men who was an expert swimmer was so moved by the imploring signals of the drowning man that he threw off his loose garments saying, "I will save that man or die with him."

He reached his fellow sailor just as he was about to take his last gulp of air. He miraculously dragged the drowning man back to the ship. He brought him so near the ship that a small boat was lowered, and both men were taken up and laid down upon the deck. The man that had been swept overboard was entirely unconscious, and his deliverer was nearly so. As the ship was rocking back and forth, the crew members tried to revive them. As soon as the rescued man opened his eyes and found he was not in the ocean, his first words were, "Who saved me?" They pointed to his deliverer, still lying on the deck in his wet clothes. He crept to his deliverer and, putting his arms around his ankles, said, "I am your servant forever! I am your servant forever!"

Child of God struggling and battling with temptation, Jesus Christ jumped overboard when your life was at its darkest hour and risked everything to save you! I do not understand the crowd that lives on the fence. Why don't we wake up and say, "Who saved me?" Find Christ's ankles and tell Him, "I am your servant forever!" The Bible says, *"No man can serve two masters: for either he will hate the one, and love the other; or else he will hold to the one, and despise the other. Ye cannot serve God and mammon"* Matthew 6:24. Are you a servant of God?

You will never defeat your nemesis, the Devil; you will never conquer your passions, lust, and pride; you will never do away with the temptations that beset you everyday until you are filled with the Scriptures, the Spirit, and the heart of a grateful, determined Servant. Pour your energies, your emotions, and your all into serving the Savior. Then you will find that you are too busy to be beset on every side (Psalms 139:5). You will outgrow your temptations because you have so much to do.

You alone and on your own have no way to escape temptation. The way of escape is not a plan but a Person. It is not something but Someone. The closer we draw to Him the closer we will be to freedom and victory of temptation.

Yield Not To Temptation
by Horatio R. Palmer

Yield not to temptation, for yielding is sin,
Each vict'ry will help you some other to win;
Fight manfully onward, dark passions subdue,
Look ever to Jesus, He will carry you through.

Shun evil companions, bad language disdain,
God's name hold in rev'rence, nor take it in vain;
Be thoughtful and earnest, kindhearted and true,
Look ever to Jesus, He will carry you through.

To him that o'ercometh God giveth a crown,
Through faith we shall conquer, though often cast down;
He who is our Saviour, our strength will renew,
Look ever to Jesus, He will carry you through

Ask the Savior to help you,
Comfort, strengthen, and keep you,
He is willing to aid you,
He will carry you through.

About the Author

Jon M. Jenkins was born on January 3, 1962, in Adrian, Michigan. He is the son of Pastor and Mrs. Howard Jenkins. Pastor Howard Jenkins began preaching in 1950. Jon grew up in a fine Christian home. His parents have faithfully served the Lord his entire life, including nearly seven years on the mission field.

In his teenage years Jon left home, and for almost three years was a prodigal son. He became heavily involved in the drug and rock 'n' roll culture. His years of straying came to a dramatic conclusion on Friday night, October 5, 1979, when Jon was gloriously saved just shy of his 18th birthday. Jon immediately turned into a raging fire for God. By the conclusion of his senior year of high school in Michigan Center, Michigan, he had led thirty-one of his public school classmates to Christ, started a high school Bible club, and become the youth director and bus director at the Maple Grove Baptist Church in Jackson, Michigan, where his father served as pastor for thirty years.

Jon surrendered to preach on Tuesday night March 17, 1980, at the First Baptist Church of Hammond, Indiana, during Pastors' School following a message by Pastor Dan Parr, who was dying with terminal cancer. In September of 1980, Jon enrolled as a freshman at Hyles-Anderson College where he met and married Deborah Annette Harris, a 1982 graduate of Hyles-Anderson College. Pastor and Mrs. Jenkins have three children, two sons and a daughter, ages 21, 18, and 16.

Upon college graduation Jon immediately became an assistant

pastor at the Evergreen Bible Baptist Church in Kalkaska, Michigan. While in this capacity, Jon served as bus, youth and children's ministries director.

In May of 1986, Pastor Jenkins moved to Gaylord, Michigan, a rural northern Michigan community of about 3,500 people, to start a new church. On the second Sunday in May 1986, the Grace Baptist Church was born. For the past 23 years the church has experienced miraculous growth. In the spring of 2008, the church averaged 1,100 in Sunday school attendance, posting a high day on May 14th of 1,573. The Sunday evening and Wednesday evening attendance is regularly over six hundred. Grace Baptist Church has become a Mecca to thousands of people across the country who love the "Old Time Religion." Over nine thousand people have walked the aisle and publicly professed faith in Christ in the brief history of this miracle church. Pastor Jenkins has led the church through six major building programs. Presently, the church owns over $5,000,000 of property, which includes a new $2,000,000 college campus. The church is in the planning and design stages of a new state-of-the-art multimillion dollar church building to be constructed as the Lord provides. The church employs seventy people, including six assistant pastors, and operates sixteen bus routes, a 24 hour-a-day fundamental Christian radio station (88.1 FM), and the Grace Baptist Christian School with an annual enrollment of over 140 students in K4-12th grades. The church also founded the Grace Baptist College in 2003, matriculating over 170 students for the 2007-2008 school year, its fifth year. In 2008 Pastor Jenkins led the church in giving $178,000 for world-wide faith promise missions. The church has helped in the starting of five area churches. Pastor

Jenkins has written a number of books. He travels extensively speaking in national conferences, holding local church revivals, church growth conferences, family conferences, camp meetings, youth conferences, and youth camps. He received an honorary Doctorate of Divinity degree from Providence Baptist College in 2001 and a Doctorate of Humanities degree from Hyles-Anderson College in 2002.

ECHOES PUBLICATIONS

Visit **www.echoespublications.com** for additional resources on the subject of spiritual victory. Dr. Jenkins delivers pointed and practical truths from God's Word that will encourage, instruct, correct, and enhance the lives of individuals and families.

**Audio Sermon series albums
include titles such as:**

1. "Dynamic Insights For Spiritual Growth"
2. "Spiritual Shipwrecks"
3. "So...You Have A Problem?"
4. "Spiritual Pitfalls"
5. "Let's Build A Church"
6. "Begotten To Hope"
7. "Slaying Your Giants"
8. "Possessing Your Vessel"

**Other books available by Dr. &
Mrs. Jenkins include:**

1. "Happy Wife, Happy Life"
2. "How Sweet It Is"
3. "Life's Good"